"Michael Genovese is among the more thoughtful and accomplished of our social scientists. No surprise, then, that this latest in his long line of books, *Building Tomorrow's Leaders Today*, is as grounded in the classics as in the contemporaneous context. The book has the advantage of being short and to the point—while providing a careful and considered framework for what leadership development in the second decade of the 21st century might look like."

—**Barbara Kellerman**, Harvard University, USA

"Michael Genovese is a terrific scholar, teacher, and storyteller on the realities of what it takes to be an effective leader. This is a superbly written, fascinating page-turner of a leadership primer—provocative and compelling!"

—**Thomas E. Cronin**, Colorado College, USA

"Only a polymath like Genovese could write a leadership book that is grounded in serious scholarship but written with a warmth and wit that welcomes all readers."

—**Joanne B. Ciulla**, Jepson School of Leadership Studies, University of Richmond, USA

"Genovese's *Building Tomorrow's Leaders Today: On Becoming a Polymath Leader* is a formidable study of the requirements of leadership. Genovese draws from a stunningly diverse range of sources to show us what true leadership is. But what's more, he shows us how great leaders can still be made. This book is as impressive as it is inspiring, and is a must for anyone interested in how leadership can work in an increasingly divided world."

—**Todd L. Belt**, Department of Political Science, University of Hawai'i at Hilo, USA

Building Tomorrow's Leaders Today

If we are to build tomorrow's leaders today, it would help if we knew what skills, temperaments, and specific competencies will be valuable as we face future needs. What will tomorrow look like? What key factors are we likely to confront tomorrow? If the past is prelude, the world of tomorrow will be characterized by rapid change, new technology, greater diversity, more globalization, and the need for lifelong learning. This book focuses on leadership; what it is, how it works, and how complex, multi-layered, and multidimensional it is. As a political scientist and presidential scholar, Michael Genovese incorporates a wide range of disciplinary perspectives and research on leadership in this book. Students, practitioners, and leadership scholars will welcome this new book and its look to the future.

Michael A. Genovese received his PhD from the University of Southern California. He currently holds the Loyola Chair of leadership studies, is a professor of political science, and director of the Institute of Leadership Studies at Loyola Marymount University in California. In 2006, he was made a fellow of Queens College, Oxford University. Professor Genovese has written over thirty books, including *The Paradoxes of the American Presidency* (with Tom Cronin; Oxford University Press, 4th edition, 2013) and *Memo to a New President: The Art and Science of Presidential Leadership* (Oxford University Press, 2008).

LEADERSHIP: RESEARCH AND PRACTICE SERIES

A James MacGregor Burns Academy of Leadership Collaboration

SERIES EDITORS

Georgia Sorenson, PhD, Research Professor in Leadership Studies, University of Maryland, and Founder of the James MacGregor Academy of Leadership and the International Leadership Association.

Ronald E. Riggio, PhD, Henry R. Kravis Professor of Leadership and Organizational Psychology and Former Director of the Kravis Leadership Institute at Claremont McKenna College.

Scott T. Allison and George R. Goethals
Heroic Leadership: An Influence Taxonomy of 100 Exceptional Individuals

Michelle C. Bligh and Ronald E. Riggio (Eds.)
Exploring Distance in Leader-Follower Relationships: When Near Is Far and Far Is Near

Michael A. Genovese
Building Tomorrow's Leaders Today: On Becoming a Polymath Leader

Michael A. Genovese and Janie Steckenrider (Eds.)
Women as Political Leaders: Studies in Gender and Governing

Jon P. Howell
Snapshots of Great Leadership

Aneil Mishra and Karen E. Mishra
Becoming a Trustworthy Leader: Psychology and Practice

Ronald E. Riggio and Sherylle J. Tan (Eds.)
Leader Interpersonal and Influence Skills: The Soft Skills of Leadership

Dinesh Sharma and Uwe P. Gielen (Eds.)
The Global Obama: Crossroads of Leadership in the 21st Century

Building Tomorrow's Leaders Today

On Becoming a Polymath Leader

MICHAEL A. GENOVESE

Routledge
Taylor & Francis Group

NEW YORK AND LONDON

First published 2014
by Routledge
711 Third Avenue, New York, NY 10017

and by Routledge
27 Church Road, Hove, East Sussex BN3 2FA

Routledge is an imprint of the Taylor & Francis Group, an informa business

Library of Congress Cataloging-in-Publication Data

Genovese, Michael A.
Building tomorrow's leaders today : on becoming a polymath leader / Michael A. Genovese.—1 Edition.
    pages cm.—(Leadership: research and practice)
 1. Leadership—Psychological aspects.   I. Title.
HD57.7.G456   2013
303.3'4—dc23   2013029019

ISBN: 978-1-84872-530-0 (hbk)
ISBN: 978-1-84872-531-7 (pbk)
ISBN: 978-1-315-85651-3 (ebk)

Typeset in Palatino
by Apex CoVantage, LLC

Printed and bound in the United States of America by Sheridan Books, Inc. (a Sheridan Group Company).

This book is dedicated to Gaby—
One love, if it is the right one, can last an eternity

CONTENTS

Series Foreword by Ronald E. Riggio and Georgia Sorenson   xi

Preface   xiii

About the Author   xvii

Chapter 1   Leadership: Too Important to Be Left to Chance   1

Chapter 2   A Leadership Composite from the Classics   37

Chapter 3   The Leadership Toolkit   49

Chapter 4   Leadership and the Crosscurrents of Change   81

Chapter 5   Building Leaders: The Genovese Leadership Academy   93

Chapter 6   Conclusion: Leadership, for What?   101

Author Index   111

Subject Index   115

SERIES FOREWORD

Leadership is fantastically complex. It involves the interaction of qualities and character of the leader, the followers and their vicissitudes, and a variety of environmental and situational factors. Renault/Nissan CEO, Carlos Ghosn, states that "the role of leadership is to transform the complex situation into small pieces and prioritize them." Michael Genovese has done just that. He has taken the complexity of leadership, acknowledged it, but has broken it down into bite-sized chunks so that any student of leadership (and that likely includes all of us) can more easily understand it. The main point of this book is both complex and simple: Leadership is complicated, but we have enough knowledge about it to instruct leaders (and would-be leaders) how to do it better.

Drawing on a wide range of literature, from the ancient Greeks, to Shakespeare, Machiavelli, and modern theorists, Genovese shows us that effective leaders, what he terms *polymath* leaders, are leaders who are broadly educated, both formally and informally, through experience, to be flexible, adaptable, and able to use many talents and tools.

What is particularly interesting about Michael Genovese's approach, and one that differentiates it from scores of books on leadership and leader development, is that he takes a *transdisciplinary* approach to the topic. A political scientist and presidential scholar, Genovese incorporates a wide range of disciplinary perspectives and research on leadership. From philosophy to psychology to lessons from classic literature, to biographies of leaders, as well as political science, Genovese pulls these seemingly divergent approaches together to form a sensible whole. He makes it look easy, in the way that a juggler or gymnast might make intricate movements appear simple.

Building Tomorrow's Leaders Today is a book with so much depth that the practicing or aspiring leader will find herself or himself returning to it time and time again for insight or practical advice on how to lead.

Ronald E. Riggio
Georgia Sorenson

PREFACE

Academically, I am a bit schizophrenic. I am trained as a political scientist who specializes in the study of the American presidency. Thus, as a scientist, I seek to reduce reality down to testable propositions and theories. My training as a political scientist has exposed me to a core belief in the discipline: That individual leaders do not matter very much.

Political science searches for testable propositions. The field reduces the world down from complex reality to simple and testable propositions. In subfields such as international relations, individual agency—leadership—is secondary to factors such as balance of power, economic strength, military superiority, national interest, and role expectations.

Being grounded in a methodology of science, my training tells me to search for broad patterns of behavior, not individual acts of leadership.

Over the years, my academic interests evolved—some might say devolved—and I was increasingly drawn from presidential studies to the field of leadership studies. In this field, leaders matter a great deal. In fact, leaders are the primary reason this field of study exists. To leadership studies professors, what the individual does, the choices made, matter.[1]

Being torn in two directions isn't as bad as one might imagine. In fact these two divergent starting points can open up rather than close one's mind. I am a prisoner of neither the cold theories of science, nor the hot input of powerful individuals. I am intrigued by leaders, the decisions they make, how they seek to lead, what it takes to lead, and why leadership is such a difficult enterprise. It is that puzzle that I am trying to address in this book.

For whom is this book written? Although it is intended for a wide audience, it will, I hope, be especially useful for students who are committed to making a difference in their communities, those wishing to rise in their organizations, and anyone wishing to improve their skills and advance their causes. It is a book designed to help you become more effective at creating and managing change.

In this book, I focus on leadership; what it is, how it works, and how you might take steps toward becoming a polymath leader. Currently, *leadership* is a growth industry, with dozens of books promising the reader a magic pill that will give you the secret to leadership excellence. If only it were that easy. The five pillars of leadership, four keys to leadership, six secrets to . . . if it were that easy, we would all have mastered it by now.[2]

No, leadership is a complex, paradoxical phenomenon that is nuanced, multilayered, and multidimensional. Good leadership does not come from a magic pill but from hard work, discipline, and focused practice.

Most universities today embrace, as part of their mission, a commitment to "producing the leaders of tomorrow." They advertise to parents and students that by graduation date, the young men and women who attend their university will be prepared to meet the challenges of tomorrow. Again, if only . . .

Most of these claims are more wind than substance. Very few universities take leadership seriously. They know that it is the flavor of the month and jump on the leadership bandwagon, yet rarely incorporate leadership seriously in the curricula.[3]

Many corporations, not-for-profits, churches, schools, even the military stress leadership training as a key to success, and some do a fine job at it. Yet most pay mere lip service to developing leaders and leadership skills.

Finally, a corps of leadership experts, consultants, coaches, and self-promoters, have arisen promising to make a silk purse out of virtually any person[4]—for the right price. Yes, there are some outstanding leadership consultants and coaches, but with this, as when going to buy a used car, *caveat emptor*—let the buyer beware.

Put together, all of these components compose what Barbara Kellerman refers to as the "leadership industry"[5] with grand claims and promises of magic elixirs. Yet, no magic pill exists. If you want to be a better leader, roll up your sleeves and get ready for hard work, very hard.

Each chapter of this book begins with a leadership quote (an epigraph) and a Genovese Leadership Theorem. A theorem is an idea that is clearly true. You may judge for yourself just how true these theorems are.

This book is the product of many years of reading, writing, teaching, and thinking hard and deeply about leadership. Several leadership scholars have been especially important to the development of my thinking on this subject: James M. Burns, Warren

Bennis, John Gardner, Peter Drucker, Niccolo Machiavelli, William Shakespeare, Plato, Aristotle, and most especially, my friend and frequent coauthor, Thomas E. Cronin. Their innovative, challenging, creative work in the field opened doors and minds and advanced our understanding of this complex field.

A bit closer to home, research assistants Matt Candau, Rebecca Hartley, Brianna Bruns, and Katherine McGrath, and the administrative assistant at the Institute for Leadership Studies at Loyola Marymount University, Mackenzie Burr, were of enormous help, and I thank them profoundly.

Most important, I wish to thank my beautiful wife Gabriela. She has given me so very many gifts over the course of our time together, but—and all scholars will understand how important this is—she has given me a very rare and special gift, the gift of guilt-free writing time! Gaby, you are the best, and I will continue to work hard to deserve you.

☐ Notes

1. See Thomas E. Cronin and Michael A. Genovese, *Leadership Matters: Unleashing the Power of Paradox* (Boulder, CO: Paradigm Publishers, 2012).
2. Beware of leadership gurus who promise a panacea. They are usually selling snake oil.
3. See J. Thomas Wren, Ronald E. Riggio, and Michael A. Genovese, *Leadership and the Liberal Arts* (New York, NY: Palgrave MacMillan, 2009).
4. Remember, an expert is a former pert.
5. Barbara Kellerman, *The End of Leadership* (New York, NY: Harper Brothers, 2012).

ABOUT THE AUTHOR

Loyola Marymount University, photo by Glenn Cratty

Michael A. Genovese received a PhD from the University of Southern California in 1979. He currently holds the Loyola Chair of leadership studies, is professor of political science, and director of the Institute for Leadership Studies at Loyola Marymount University. In 2006, he was made a fellow at Queens College, Oxford University. Professor Genovese has written over thirty books, including *The Paradoxes of the American Presidency* (coauthored by Thomas E. Cronin, Oxford University Press, 4th edition, 2013); *The Presidency and the Challenges of Democracy* (coedited with Lori Cox Han, Palgrave, 2006); *The Presidency and Domestic Policy* (with William W. Lammers, CQ Press, 2000); *The Power of the American Presidency 1789–2000* (Oxford University Press, 2001); *The Presidential Dilemma* (Transaction, 3rd edition, 2011); *The Encyclopedia of the American Presidency* (winner of the New York Public Library "Best of Reference" work of 2004; Facts-on File, 2nd edition, 2010); *Memo to a New President: The Art and Science of Presidential Leadership* (Oxford University Press, 2008); *Contending Approaches to the American Presidency* (CQ Press, 2012); and *Leadership Matters* (with Thomas E. Cronin, Paradigm Publishers, 2012; winner of the Outstanding Leadership Book of the Year award, presented at the 2013 International Leadership Association meeting). He has also written a cookbook, *Me and Mach: Food Fit for The Prince* (ebook), *Women as Political Leaders* (Taylor and Francis, edited with Janie Steckenrider, 2013), and *Shakespeare and Politics* (Paradigm Publishers, edited with Bruce Althusler, forthcoming). His articles and reviews have appeared in the *American Political Science Review, The Times Literary Supplement, Public Opinion Quarterly, Presidential Studies Quarterly, White House Studies, The Journal of*

Leadership Studies, and elsewhere. Genovese has won over a dozen university and national teaching awards, including the Fritz B. Burns Distinguished Teaching Award (1995) and the Rains Excellence in Research Award (2011). Professor Genovese frequently appears as a commentator on local and national television. He is also associate editor of the journal, *White House Studies,* is on the editorial board of the journals, *Rhetoric & Public Affairs,* and the *International Leadership Journal,* has lectured for the United States Embassy abroad, and is editor of Palgrave Macmillan's, "The Evolving American Presidency" book series. Professor Genovese has been the Washington Center's "scholar-in-residence" at three Democratic national political conventions and the 2008 presidential inauguration, and served as "scholar-in-residence" at the 2012 Republican national convention. In 2004–2005, Professor Genovese served as president of the Presidency Research Group of the American Political Science Association. He is currently on the advisory boards of the Washington Center, The Center for the Study of Los Angeles, and the Foundation for International Education.

CHAPTER 1

Leadership

Too Important to Be Left to Chance

It is change, continuing change, inevitable change, that is the dominant factor in society today. No sensible decision can be made any longer without taking into account not only the world as it is, but the world as it will be . . . this in turn means that our statesmen, our businessmen, our everyman must take on a science fictional way of thinking.

—Isaac Asimov

Genovese Leadership Theorem: Leadership is aspirational or it is nothing.

Nearly a century ago, the German sociologist Max Weber asked a question that vexes us still: "What kind of a man [person] must one be if he is to be allowed to put his hand on the wheel of history?"

Weber's answer?

"One can say that three preeminent qualities are decisive for the politician: passion, a feeling of responsibility, and a sense of proportion."

He goes on to explain:

To be sure, mere passion, however genuinely felt, is not enough. It does not make a politician, unless passion as devoted to a "cause" also makes responsibility to this cause the guiding star of action. And for this, a sense of proportion is needed. This is the decisive psychological quality of the politician: his ability to let realities work upon him with inner concentration and calmness. Hence his *distance* to things and men. "Lack of distance" *per se* is one of the deadly sins of every politician. [. . .] the problem is simply how can warm passion and a cool sense of proportion be forged together in one and the same soul? Politics is made with the head, not with other parts of the body or soul. And yet devotion to politics, if it is not to be frivolous intellectual play but rather genuinely human conduct, can be born and nourished from passion alone. However, that firm taming of the soul, which distinguishes the passionate politician and differentiates him from the "sterilely excited" and mere political dilettante, is possible only through habituation to detachment in every sense of the word. The "strength" of a political "personality" means, in the first place, the possession of these qualities of passion, responsibility, and proportion. [. . .] the politician inwardly has to overcome a quite trivial and all-too-human enemy: a quite vulgar vanity, the deadly enemy of all matter-of-fact devotion to a cause, and of all distance, in this case, of distance towards one's self.[1]

Must we, as Vladimir and Estragon do, merely wait for Godot,[2] or can we create the leaders of tomorrow, develop and train men and women in the skills and temperament needed to guide us in a dangerous and uncertain world?[3]

Plato enjoined us to do so. He believed that extended, concentrated leadership training was a necessary precondition to good governing. His *Philosopher-King* would go through years of rigorous study in preparation for assuming power. Plutarch, in his parallel lives of influential Greeks and Romans invited us to learn the lessons of both positive and negative role models. Likewise, Niccolo Machiavelli's *The Prince* was an effort to advise a would-be ruler on how to govern wisely and well, learning from the great and infamous leaders of the past. Plato, Plutarch, and Machiavelli believed—knew—that leadership was an art as well as a science, and that to govern with skill, a ruler must be well-trained in the specialized craft of governing. Positions of leadership were no place for inexperienced amateurs.

Of course, this view challenges the widely believed myth that leaders are born, not made. Yes, we are born with genes that predispose us in various directions, but there is no leadership gene that propels one to the heights of power and authority. Nature matters, but nurture matters more. Our childhood experiences, leadership opportunities as we grow, education, and a variety of other developmental factors help make us leaders—if we choose to move in that direction. Therefore, we ask: what factors help lead one toward effective leadership? What steps can be taken along the way, to transform person X into a better leader?

Elsewhere, my frequent coauthor Thomas E. Cronin and I listed some common myths about leadership:

- Leaders are born, not made.
- Leadership is a rare and uncommon talent.
- Leaders are necessarily charismatic.
- Leadership is found only at the top of an organization.
- Office holders are necessarily leaders.
- Organizational or group members are either leaders or followers.
- Leaders are smarter and more creative than most of us.
- Power is the dominant currency of leadership.[4]

So just who should have their hand on the wheel of history? Someone who can turn that wheel in the right direction. And what type of person is most likely to both know the right direction toward which to turn that wheel *and* have the experience, the training, the skill, the courage, and the temperament to actually turn the wheel? A polymath leader.

Do we merely sit back and wait, hoping that our savior will arrive, or do we self-consciously set out to develop men and women with the skill, insight, values, compassion, integrity, and strength to turn the wheel? Of course, we do not merely hope, we also work. And becoming an excellent leader, a proficient leader, takes long, hard work.

An old Arab proverb, apropos to the West as well, goes: "As you are so will be the rulers that rule you." Or, as a similar saying has it: "In a democracy, people tend to get the government they deserve." Although it may seem convenient to sit back and wait for a leader to save us, or blame them when they fail us, the reality is that sometimes we do end up with the leaders we deserve. And usually we deserve better.

From the time humans began to live in communities, leadership became necessary. All organizations and communities require direction, coordination, and leadership. A hundred years ago, sociologist Robert Michels coined the phrase, "the iron law of oligarchy," in reference to the fact that in all organizations, leaders emerge.[5] It is an iron law that some type of oligarchy or elite will run things. And a study of human history confirms this iron law that leaders are indispensable, inevitable, and ubiquitous. They can also be very dangerous.

But what makes leadership so necessary? Leadership scholar Michael Harvey argues that the human condition does. He writes,

Leadership is part and parcel of the human condition. A mystery as modern as the nation-state and as ancient as the tribe, it brings together the best and worst in human nature: love and hate, hope and fear, trust and deceit, service and selfishness. Leadership draws on who we are, but it also shapes what we might be—a kind of alchemy of souls that can produce both Lincoln's "better angels of our nature" and Hitler's willing executioners. In its constituent parts leadership includes three basic social organizing patterns—kinship, reciprocity, and command. From kinship it draws a sense of connection (if often exploited) between leaders and followers. From reciprocity it draws a sense of mutual exchange and benefit (if often betrayed). But from command it takes its most visible aspect, for leadership is above all a social relation of dominance and consent (if often constrained), yoked uneasily together. At the heart of leadership is a tension precipitated by our double nature— social animals with self-reflective and often selfish minds.[6]

Humans need organization as well as hierarchy. As soon as our ancestors started living in groups, government became necessary. And as soon as government became necessary, leaders became necessary. Collective work requires coordination, thus government and leadership.

☐ The Polymath Leader

The leader of the twenty-first century must be a master of many talents; he or she must be a *polymath leader.* And just what is a polymath leader?

The *American Heritage Dictionary* defines *polymath* as "a person of great and varied learning."[7] Such a person must learn a great deal about a great many things.

The United States Army, which has one of the world's most sophisticated leadership training programs, tries to create what it calls a "panathlete" leader. This is the ideal leader and is defined as officers "who are not only competent in their core warrior skills, but who are also scholars; men and women who are creative, innovative, strategically-minded, culturally competent, and skilled in all aspects of peace, war, politics, and civil administration."[8]

To illustrate, there are many polymaths throughout history with whom you are already familiar. *Aristotle* (384–322 BCE) of Greece, engaged in philosophy, physics, metaphysics, poetry, rhetoric, logic, politics and government, ethics, biology, zoology, and more. The famous Roman emperor, *Julius Caesar* (100–44 BCE) was another polymath leader. He was an accomplished orator, writer, general, manager, strategist, and much more. *Jafar Al-Sadig* (702–765 CE) from Medina, in Saudi Arabia, was an Islamic scholar, Iman, astronomer, philosopher, physician, physicist, and jurist. *Al-Jazari* (1136–1204) was a Kurdish astronomer, mathematician, Islamic scholar, innovator, and mechanical engineer.

Theodore Roosevelt was a polymath. Soldier, statesman, president, author, cowboy, hunter, explorer, Roosevelt was a well-rounded, accomplished, and multitalented person. Perhaps the best known and most accomplished polymath is *Leonardo da Vinci* (1452–1519) of Florence, Italy. Leonardo was a sculptor, painter, military strategist, inventor, scientist, mathematician, physicist, engineer, humanist cartographer, and poet. *Isaac Newton* (1643–1727) was a British physicist, mathematician, astronomer, and theologian. *Thomas Jefferson* (1743–1826) was a philosopher, inventor, statesman, diplomat, horticulturalist, architect, president, and author of the Declaration of Independence.

It is this polymath leader that president-elect John F. Kennedy spoke of just prior to his inauguration:

> When at some future date the high court of history sits in judgment on each one of us . . . our success or failure in whatever office we hold will be measured by our answers to four questions:
>
> Were we truly men of courage . . .?
> Were we truly men of integrity . . .?
> Were we truly men of judgment . . .?
> Were we truly men of dedication . . .?"[9]

☐ Defining Leadership

Leadership scholars often bemoan the fact that there is no single agreed-upon definition of leadership. But we should not fret. First, many fields offer contested definitions of just what it is they study. In my own field, political science, there is no consensus on just what we mean by *politics*. Second, there is enough general agreement on the component parts of leadership that we do know what it is we study, and that agreement animates both research and understanding. The obsession with definitional purity obscures rather than enlightens our understanding as we digress to argue just how many angels can dance on the head of a pin.

The *American Heritage Dictionary* defines *leader* as "one that leads," an altogether useless definition. But this same dictionary defines *lead* as "to show the way," a surprisingly apt if incomplete definition. Leaders show the way. They may or may not be office holders. Martin Luther King, Jr. held no political office, but he certainly showed us the way. The dictionary also defines *lead* as "to guide," another apt definition. Leaders guide us. And they do so much more. They set a vision, move the machinery of government or the organization behind the achievement of that vision, mobilize supporters, recruit others to their cause, organize, direct, perhaps inspire, set strategy, educate, coach, persuade, teach, influence, and help us achieve group goals.

I often ask new CEOs, new college presidents, even new student body presidents, "What three things do you hope to achieve by the end of your term?" I pick three for no good reason other than it forces the new leader to identify the things that are most important. You would be amazed at how few new leaders can answer this question. They fumble and mumble, and it soon becomes clear they are in it for all the wrong reasons. Goal-oriented leaders, leaders who use their influence and power to *do something*, can answer that question in a heartbeat. They are there to achieve specific goals, to make things happen, to get things done.

Broken down to the component parts, we know that leadership is:

- A *process*
- that involves leaders *and* followers
- who engage in a *relationship* of *influence* and *trust*
- where leaders help *mobilize* the *group* and *inspire* them (true leadership is aspirational)
- to achieve *mutually desired goals*.

Having both a personal and a public role connects the leader to the community or organization, and although the leader thinks he or she should be at the head of the parade, the leader must always remember that a parade is a group exercise involving leader and followers. This creates a symbiotic relationship between the leader and led, the individual and the community. You can't have one without the other.

☐ The Metaphysics of Leadership

Philosophers have a difficult time defining what they mean by *metaphysics*. The word derives from fourteen books written by Aristotle, which came to be referred to as "Aristotle's Metaphysics."

Generally the word refers to the core or fundamental nature of something; that which does not change. Aristotle himself referred to "being as such" and "first causes." From this, we can understand metaphysics to mean "first and unchanging principles."

So what are the first and unchanging principles of leadership?

(1) In all communities and organizations, *leadership is necessary.*
(2) Leadership can *inspire, empower*, and *elevate* yet it can also *enslave, degrade*, and *damage.*
(3) Because unchecked power *does* often corrupt and because all leadership is potentially dangerous, we must be careful to encase leaders in some check and balance system.
(4) We *sell ourselves short* when we *rely too heavily on leaders to solve our problems.*
(5) Leadership is *too important to be left to inexperienced amateurs.*

☐ Great Man Theory versus Forces of History: Agency and Causation in Leadership Studies

Just how important are leaders? Thomas Carlyle believed that great men, or heroes, made history.[10] Larger-than-life figures such as Moses, Jesus, Napoleon, and Lincoln imposed the force of their will upon reality and changed the world. Carlyle believed that "every institution is the lengthened shadow of a great man."[11] In sharp contrast, Ralph Waldo Emerson believed that "Events are in the saddle and ride mankind."

In contrast to Carlyle's view is Leo Tolstoy, who believed that social and historical forces larger than mere individuals mattered most.[12] Tolstoy savagely rebuts Carlyle's view, arguing that leaders are the "playthings of massive forces that move history toward unknown and predetermined ends."[13]

To Tolstoy, leaders ride waves; to Carlyle, leaders make waves. Tolstoy believed that the forces of history shaped and determined the actions of leaders; Carlyle believed it was leaders who shaped and determined history. Steven Sample, former president of the University of Southern California, takes the middle ground on this controversy:

It may well be that our world is largely Tolstoyan, subject to historical forces which no man or woman can fully measure and analyze, and the consequences of which no person can fully predict. Thus, to that extent, leaders are in fact history's slaves. Yet, Carlyle's able man can indeed have a lasting impact on the world; that historical determinism is never totally in control.[14]

Like Steven Sample, we take a middle ground view of agency and causation. Change is a function of multiple causes. As James M. Burns has written, the only thing we really know is that "none of us, no general, no leader, could control events. Indeed, even the greatest king was only 'history's slave'."[15] Abraham Lincoln, in an April 4, 1864, letter to Albert G. Hodges, supports this view. "I claim," he wrote, "not to have controlled events, but confess plainly that events have controlled me." And yet, if events set for Lincoln and other leaders, parameters of action, they were not straight-jackets that tightly bound the leader. There was still *choice* involved. As Norman Provizer has written, "Events control actions by providing parameters that shape and channel choice. Yet the leader instead of being 'history's slave' is in actuality history's servant."[16] Or, as Alexis de Toqueville reminds us in his classic work, *Democracy in America*, "Providence did not make mankind entirely free or completely enslaved. Providence has, in truth, drawn a predetermined circle around each man beyond which he cannot pass; but within those case limits man is strong and free, and so are people."[17]

Further, Karl Marx noted that "Men make their own history, but they do not make it just as they please, they do not make it under circumstances chosen by themselves, but under circumstances directly encountered, given and transmitted from the past."[18]

Leaders make choices, but these choices are not free of outside forces. Context is important, and the context helps define choice. We are all creatures of circumstance, and yet, circumstances are not so prescribed as to leave no room for choice. Within these circumstances, leaders can make good or bad choices.[19] Leaders do have a say in outcomes, and yet their choices are still enveloped within context. President James Buchanan, faced with a coming Civil War, made several bad choices; Abraham Lincoln, faced with a Civil War, made many good (and a few bad) choices.[20]

Dean Keith Simonton puts the Carlyle versus Tolstoy controversy to the test, examining whether the forces of history or the actions of great men determine history. After an exhaustive study, Simonton concludes—not surprisingly—that both schools of thought "have some merit," and that the argument, when played out in reality, "is much too complicated to assign victory to either theorist," and Tolstoy and Carlyle "have fought to a draw."[21]

Thus, we are left to study the leader in context. The leader neither rises above nor is he the helpless slave of context; it is an interactive process. As Provizer notes, "Just as the leader cannot totally obliterate context, neither can context completely eliminate the impact of the leader."

Leaders do not create the movement and forces of history that make up the context in which they attempt to lead. They take what is given and work within this context, even as they may try to change or break out of the binding forces of that context.

□ Building Tomorrow's Leaders Today

If we are to build tomorrow's leaders, today, it would help if we knew what skills, temperaments, and specific competencies will be valuable as we face future needs. What will tomorrow look like? What key factors are we likely to confront tomorrow?[22]

I would argue that the world of tomorrow will be characterized by:

(1) Rapid change
(2) New technology
(3) Greater diversity
(4) More integration and greater interdependence and connectivity
(5) More globalization (world without borders)
(6) More widespread access to information
(7) The slow decline of national sovereignty and rise of cross-border collaboration
(8) The need for more multilateralism
(9) The need for greater flexibility
(10) Lifelong learning

Or, put more succinctly, globalization is dramatically changing the leadership landscape.

□ Leadership and the Pressures of Globalization

So much of leadership is about helping the group adapt to change. In the future, this will be accomplished less by managing change, and more by adjusting to change. And change will occur at an unprecedented pace. The next generation of leaders will—by necessity—be change leaders.

The familiar, the stable, the tried-and-true, will all recede as fast-paced change overtakes the status quo, forcing us to adjust and adapt. If we aren't comfortable and prepared for change, our lives will be confused, confusing, and difficult.

This rapid-fire change will be difficult for individuals, organizations, and nations. And it is hard—even through the lens of science fiction—to see with any certainty what our lives and world will be like in twenty-five years. Utopia? Probably not. Distopia? Possibly. Unless we develop leaders and followers capable of adjusting constructively to change.

We are entering a new era of governance and leadership. This new epoch is having a profound effect on the way governance is practiced and on how leadership is exercised. We are now entering a more globalized, interconnected, and interdependent world. Globalization is a process by which the connections between people, states, and regions become more pronounced and important. Driven largely by market forces and emerging technological innovations, it is changing the way we exercise leadership.[23]

This new age will have a profound impact on the way leaders will lead. In the past, *power* has often been associated with a strong leader commanding or compelling constituents to follow. Possessing the authoritative use of force, leaders could often bark out orders and expect compliance. Even in democracies, where leaders mixed command with persuasion, leaders expected followers to fall in line. However, in this new age, leaders will be stripped of much of their power as the tools of influence (e.g., social networking) spread to a wider audience, and smaller players (e.g., Wikileaks) challenge conventional leaders for agenda control as well as public attention.[24]

Today and into the future, very few of the world's pressing problems can be solved by national policies alone. Almost every major problem facing the world now demands global solutions. From pollution, to terrorism, the spread of infectious diseases to economic development, today no nation is an island; we are all interconnected.[25]

The need to reach multinational agreements to meet pressing needs will of course, undermine the authority of the nation-state. It will further undermine the authority of national leaders.

Social and political problems no longer respect the limits of national borders. Problems from the spread of infectious diseases, to pollution, to drugs, to migration, to trade, to . . . , to nearly every social and political problem, are almost all international issues that will require multilateral solutions. The nation-state and national sovereignty are giving way to a form of internationalism that will require a new form of leadership. We are truly in an interdependent world, and globalization—like it or not—is the emerging reality. This puts new stresses on leadership, establishes new contexts for decision-making, and requires a replacement for current conceptions of leadership.

Information spread, technological innovations, the new impact of computers in an information age, will put new stresses on governments. In effect, the world will be able to think out loud. Governments will be less able to control the flow of ideas and information (as the popular uprising—Arab Spring—in 2011 in the Middle East demonstrates), and for the first time, we will be approaching a truly global village.

In a world with growing levels of uncertainty, increasing threats, rapid change, greater ambiguity, leaders will need to move with speed and be highly flexible.

The United States is the world's only superpower. With military might second to none (the United States spends more for defense than the next top 15 nations—combined!), a massive economy (the U.S. economy is larger than the next three—Japan, Great Britain, and Germany—combined!), and cultural penetration to all other parts of the globe (I defy you to go to any large city in any country in the world and not find a local child wearing a New York Yankees baseball cap or a Michael Jordan (#23) basketball jersey, or find a McDonald's or a Starbucks), the United States is *the* hegemonic power, or the "big kid on the block." But if we are so strong, why do we seem so weak? Why, at a time when there are no true rivals to power, is our grip on international events so fragile and tenuous?

The Cold War era demanded a heroic presidency. However, when the Soviet Union imploded, marking the end of the Cold War, analysts wondered what international regime would replace the old order, and presidency scholars wondered whether the imperial presidency had run its course. For a time, policy makers groped for an answer. George Bush (the first), in response to the invasion of Kuwait by Iraq, developed a multinational coalition based on a "new world order." But as the Gulf War ended, Bush abandoned this promising approach to international order and stability.

It was not until the Clinton years that the parameters of the new regime would come into view. Called globalization, it encompassed an international acceptance of global capitalism: market economies, open markets, free trade, multilateralism and integration, and interdependence. Building on the institutions designed to oversee, coordinate, and stabilize the post World War II international economy—the International Monetary Fund (IMF), the World Bank, and the General Agreement on Tariffs and Trade (GATT, now the World Trade Organization [WTO])—these institutions have, for better or worse, helped create a more integrated international economy.

The promise of globalism is political (countries that are connected by common bonds may better cooperate) and economic (a rising tide lifts all boats—critics argue that the rising tide only lifts yachts!). Those opposing the rise of globalism fear the widening gap between rich and poor nations, environmental degradation, and a decline in worker's rights.

In this age of globalization, what role and power would be assumed by the United States? And what role and power would be assumed by our leaders? Are we, in short, entering a *post-heroic* age of the presidency? Globalism takes power out of the hands of nations and places it in the hands of the market, corporations, and nongovernmental actors. National sovereignty is diminished as the requirements of the global economy drive policy. Globalism demands that market forces shape policy.[26] Thus, governments must please the international market or decline.

The United States is the most powerful actor in this system and draws benefits from its leadership position. But this new system inhibits the freedom of a president to choose. Bound by the demands of a global economy, and the need to develop multinational responses to a variety of problems, the president is less free to pursue policies he chooses and increasingly compelled to succumb to the demands of the market and to other governmental and nongovernmental actors. Going at it alone increasingly becomes a less and less attractive option.

In this new age of globalization, problems will cross national boundaries and be less amendable to strictly national solutions. The spread of weapons, nuclear and biological, the flow of refugees, environmental problems, pandemics, the international drug trade, and a host of other problems will need to be addressed via international agreements and cooperation. We are accustomed to presidents leading the nation; now they are compelled to lead in the development of international agreements to solve complex global problems. If anything, ours is an over-connected world. A crisis in Greece, or Spain, or Mexico, could have a profound effect on all other nations. Truly, we are all in it together.

In short, the world will become more high flux, and we need to build citizens and leaders who are more high flex. We will need people who can readily adapt to rapid change; people trained to move with change. We will need generalists who are nimble and able to go with the flow, even as they try to tame the flow.

Tomorrow's leaders need to be more nimble and flexible. They will need to see that the glass is half full, while realizing that the glass is constantly changing shape. The creative arts, thinking outside the box, and those who are outsiders may have skills and the appropriate temperament to navigate in this new environment. Abnormal may well become the new normal.[27]

It is often the boundary-spanning or marginal person[28] who is able to see that the emperor has no clothes, or is able to take a fresh look at a situation. Those who have suffered loss, were outcasts, spent time away, etc. may see the world with new eyes, not wedded to the status quo.

The 2011 air strike of Libya may be an example—as well as a recognition—of this new world order. The United States participated in, yet did not lead this military effort. And although it was not a joint effort of equals, it did serve as a model for the cooperative action where the United States took part in, yet did not wholly direct action.

A compelling example of the changing nature of leadership can be seen in the October 2012 struggle over the Greek debt crisis. As Greece approached the deadline of debt repayment, the leaders of Europe scrambled for a solution. The United States played a decidedly backseat role on this issue, preferring, as it did in the bombing mission in Libya, to let Europe lead from the front.

The stakes could not have been higher. If some stop-gap solution could not be reached, the stability, even the future of the Euro, was in doubt. A Wagnerian *pas de deux* unfolded as the United States began to get more and more involved, and pushed Europe to act, but the European leaders seemed unable to agree on what to do. The Euro crisis was a global issue, yet it was Europe's moment.

Germany's Angela Merkel emerged as the lynchpin of action, the only leader capable of brokering a deal. And in the end, at the eleventh hour, she was able to build a loose and fragile coalition of European governments to save (for a time at least) the Greek economy and rescue the European Union. If Greece fell, Europe would fall; if Europe fell, the United States would tumble down as well. In the modern world, the game of dominos best symbolizes the interconnection of the global community.

☐ Globalism and Democratic Distemper

Globalism is a two-edged sword. It brings some economic benefits but imposes further limits on choice. Nongovernmental organizations, international institutions, central banks, and market focuses gain in power. Nations—and the U.S. president, will lose power.

Citizens in the United States will not welcome these changes. Leaders in the United States will equally be made uncomfortable. After all, the Big Dog never welcomes a loss of authority. But these changes are inevitable, and the leader who can best make peace with the whirlwind of change, who can define the future for the American voter, who can diagnose the current malady for an unwary public and prescribe a package of policies to cope with the changing world, has a chance to constructively lead the United States—and much of the world—into this new era.[29]

In 2010 and 2011, the world witnessed significant protest in Great Britain and the United States (the Occupy Wall Street movement). In the Middle East, Arab Spring of 2011 utterly transformed the region. These *leaderless movements*, as they were called, sprang up from the frustrations of average people who felt unrepresented, oppressed, and alienated from their political systems.[30]

Conventional leaders, they felt, did not represent them nor did they address their needs and concerns. This is not an uncommon or exceptional situation in either democratic or nondemocratic states. But what we are witnessing—especially in democratic systems—is average citizens who feel they are victims, not masters of their futures. Past citizens may have merely had the illusion of control, but such perceptions cemented their attachments to the status quo.

Increasingly, political leaders will be unable to satisfy the demands of their citizenry because some of the power to shape events will be slipping through their hands. This will ratchet up the pressures on leaders while also increasing the instability of most regimes. If they can't deliver, how can they insure stability and order?

This could lead to any one of several unappealing scenarios: (1) social instability, where disgruntled citizens disrupt and threaten regime stability; (2) high leadership turnover, where voters, dissatisfied with their leaders, throw the ins out and put outs in; (3) search for a savior, where social instability leads to the rise of extremist candidates with grand promises, simple solutions, leading to dangerous consequences; or (4) a solution to fit the problems, where skilled leaders emerge to help shepherd the international system through these difficult times.

Even if scenario four emerges, it will take some time to make the transition to this new era of governing, and not all regimes will make that transition smoothly. In such difficult times, might the international system be more vulnerable to wars and social conflict? Might democratic governments face political challenges to the point of system breakdown? Can the center hold?

This epochal change will have dramatic consequences for society, politics, and leadership. Will this new age liberate us, or make us slaves to a new master? In this trend from hierarchy to leveling, will a truly more open, democratic egalitarian world emerge? Or are we to continue to be bound by Hume's painful reminder: The few always find ways to govern the many?

New challenges confront us as we look to the future in a more globalized world. One of the key dilemmas we must confront revolves around the changing nature of leadership in an age of globalization. Can leaders lead? How must we—and our leaders—change to meet the demands of this new era?

The old order is collapsing. The old ways of thinking and operating are no longer functional. The test of our nation and ourselves will be seen in how well—or poorly—we are able to adjust to this new age. Will we be masters or victims to the new age of globalism? Can our leaders devise and implement effective adaptation strategies? Will we adjust and lead, or will we stubbornly resist and decline? To effectively meet these challenges, we need to build tomorrow's leaders, today.

☐ The Who and the Why?

Why would anyone want the headaches and heartbreaks of being a leader? In many ways, it is a thankless job, fraught with perils.

Perhaps it will help to view the motivations for being a leader as a series of dichotomous variables, portrayed as a continuum. The key variables are: *self* versus *service*; to *do something* versus *be someone*; to *make up for* versus *make something happen*; and to seek *honor and recognition* versus *accomplish goals*. Graphically, these dyadic relationships could be represented as shown in Figure 1.1.

Obviously, individuals who fall toward the left pursue leadership positions for the right reasons, whereas those clustered to the right are in it for the wrong reasons. Because leaders largely self-select, one should always be a bit suspicious of those who appear too anxious to lead, too willing to assume the reins of power. As Plato writes, "The measure of a man is what he does with power."

Psychologist David McLelland saw three sources of motivation in people. First is the hunger for *power*; second is the need to *affiliate*; and third is the drive for *achievement*.[31] The founders of the American republic saw the hunger for *honor* as the primary motivator. Each has its good and bad sides, and those who master or control these drives can be both successful and happy. The key, as Aristotle reminds us, is in moderation.

Truly effective leaders just *seem* different. They possess a gravitas, a confidence, an air of casual self-assurance. Others recognize

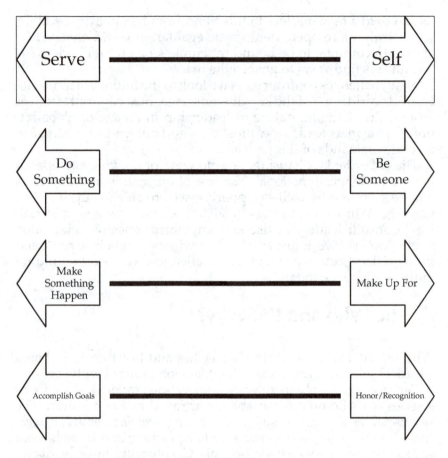

FIGURE 1.1 Motivations for Leading

this. The ancient Romans had a word for it: *Auctoritas*, the respect given to an accomplished Roman, usually from his great deeds but also from his honored lineage, service to Rome, and the way he carried himself.

The drive to gain power and position sometimes leaves the would-be leader so focused on attaining office that they lose sight of why they are running in the first place. This dilemma was powerfully brought home in the 1972 movie *The Candidate*. In that film, charismatic incumbent challenger for a U.S. Senate seat Bill McKay (played by actor Robert Redford, who bears a striking resemblance to this book's author) gets closer and closer to an upset victory, and as he does so, he jettisons deeply-held policy positions along the way, until finally he pulls off the upset and is left dumbfounded. His father, the cynical ex-governor enters the room and whispers in McKay's ear, "Son, you're a politician" in a voice so sinister one can almost see devil's horns growing on his head. Later, turning to his campaign manager, McKay asks: "What should we do now?"

Indeed, what does one do now? It is actually a more profound and complicated question than one might think. The answer depends on a variety of factors. First, what do you *want* to do? What are your goals? What is your vision for the future? Second, what *needs* to be done? President Obama came into office wanting to pass health care reform legislation; he *needed* also to boost the economy and lower the unemployment rate. Third, what *resources* are at your disposal? Fourth, what *powers* are available to you? Fifth, what *skills* do you bring to the office? Sixth, what *experiences* can guide you? And seventh, what is the *context* in which you are leading?

☐ To Seek Power or Leadership?

The words *leadership* and *power* are sometimes used interchangeably, but the words mean very different things. Leadership, the subject of this book, is about *influence*; power is about *command*. Leaders inspire and persuade; power wielders order compliance. Leaders induce followership; powerholders compel or enforce acceptance. Officeholders have power merely by virtue of occupying an office. Leaders, on the other hand, must *earn* followership. Leadership is a process of influence wherein the leader helps guide the group toward the attainment of some mutually desirable good. Power is the ability to command or force compliance in an area of recognized authority (see Table 1.1).

Power is often *positional* and attaches to an office or position, and is dependent on occupying that office in order to be effective. General Norman Schwarzkopf, who commanded the coalition forces in the first Persian Gulf War, said after leaving the military, "Seven months ago I could give a single command and 541,000 people would immediately obey it. Today I can't get a plumber to come to my house."

But power is also *personal*; that is, it is attached to the skills and attributes of an individual. The position *and* the person—the former suggests *power*, the latter suggests *leadership*.

All great leaders have a finely tuned *power sense*; that is, they are, as Machiavelli noted, consumed with and constantly focused on the accumulation and uses of power. They know what power is, how to get it, and how to use it; they know how to play one interest

TABLE 1.1 Characteristics of Leaders, Managers, and Power Wielders*

Power	Management	Leadership
Commands	Administrative Rules	Persuades
Force	Sanctions	Influence
Orders	Tells	Sells
Expects	Procedures	Motivates
Fear	Routines	Hope/Inspire
Subjects	Subordinates	Followers
Control	Stability	Change
Orders Compliance	Manages Process	Leads People
Now	Short Term	Long Term
His/Her Will	Process	Vision
Commands Action	Plans Details	Sets Direction
Transactional	Transactional	Transforming
Recognized Power	Bureaucratic Authority	Personal Appeal
Use People	Structure People	Empower People
Makes His Own Lines	Draws Within the Lines	Draws Outside the Lines
My Way or the Highway	Incentives	Inspires/Aspirational
What He Wants	Procedure	Goal Setting
Now	Today	The Future
Do What I Say	Do Things Right	Do the Right Thing
You Must	Routinize	Energize/Mobilize
e.g., Patton	Robert M. Gates	M. L. King

* Adapted from Cronin and Genovese, *Leadership Matters* (Boulder, CO: Paradigm Publishers, 2012), p. 59.

off another and how to self-promote and self-dramatize. They are people who love to poke the fire. And they want to be the ones who do the poking.

"Power," said Henry Adams, "is poison." And as Lord Acton reminded us, "Power corrupts. Absolute power corrupts absolutely." True. But power is also a way to get things done.[32]

☐ Happy People Do Not Make History

If you are happy and well adjusted, the status quo probably works just fine for you. Why change things when they are going so well? Ah, but if you are dissatisfied, a little (or a lot) angry, if you have a few rough edges, you might be more willing to envision and work for a different—better—future.

Being toxic is dangerous, yet being "a little bit different" may be a necessary precondition for change leadership. Happy people may manage well, and at times they may even lead well, but they are usually too linked to the status quo to be very effective change agents. Malcontents, on the other hand, often hunger for change.

"The pursuit of happiness" . . . It's right there in our Declaration of Independence. We have an unalienable *right* to pursue happiness. *Pursue. Not necessarily attain.*

And yet, the old French proverb reminds us, "Happy people do not make history." Leaders, people who make a difference, tend not to be happy or content. They see problems and try to correct them; see injustice and seek to reverse it; see wrongs and try to right them.

Are leaders happy? Many are *fulfilled* and *satisfied*, but that relates to their ability to accomplish goals. Most leaders have rough personal edges; they can be *ornery* and *demanding, self-centered* and *contrarian*. They are rarely "happy." But then, perhaps happiness is overrated, in leaders at least. As one wag commented, "You show me a happy leader and I'll show you a failed leader."

Many leaders had troubled or difficult childhoods, enduring tragedy, or abandonment. Many were deprived of expected parental love, lost a parent early in life, or came from a broken home.

Lincoln's depression, FDR's polio, Helen Keller's blindness, the racism that animated Martin Luther King, Jr.'s reform efforts, Steve Jobs being forced out at Apple before returning a few years later, all set these leaders apart from the norm, and compelled these determined people to reimagine the world and to reshape it.

Leaders, agents of change, are almost always slightly off kilter. They are often upset and dissatisfied. They are a little ticked off. This makes sense as happy people—those pleased or content with life—have few reasons to agitate for change, get their hands dirty with the change process, and take the time away from their happy lives to devote countless hours to working for a different tomorrow.

Even those leaders who are in it for the right reasons often feel agitated, even outraged, at injustice or inequality. So happy people do not make history—or very good leaders—because they are too busy being happy to devote their lives to the messy and time-consuming work of advancing change.

This is not to say that working to help the poor, dispossessed, hurt, excluded, or disadvantaged doesn't make one feel good.

Indeed, it should and it does. But that reverses the cause-effect calculus. You help others, *then* you feel good about it. But those who already feel good usually spend less time in the ditches doing the dirty work required to promote change.

Also, happy people generally make lousy decision makers. They are so optimistic that they expect the best, expect things to "work out," and, therefore, usually do not engage in the heavy lifting required to make sound, thoughtful decisions. They are notoriously bad at estimating probability because they just plain expect everything to work out for the best.

Slightly depressed people, on the other hand, take decision making more seriously and are much more likely to do their due diligence.

So in our search for effective leaders, (1) avoid *happy* people; (2) avoid *toxic* people; and (3) seek out slightly depressed introverts—they are the hope of humankind. Seek out the slightly discontented, the person who is slightly agitated. These people may not be happy, but they are often *fulfilled* and lead *meaningful* lives.

So "two cheers" for the pursuit of happiness in your personal life. Leaders, however, look for something else: accomplishment.

☐ Our Clashing Demands

Elsewhere, Tom Cronin and I discuss a series of clashing or contradictory expectations we have regarding leaders and leadership:

- We want decent, just, compassionate, and moral leaders, yet at times we admire and need tough, assertive, cunning, manipulative, and even intimidating leaders.
- Effective leadership involves self-confidence, fearless optimism, and the audacity of hope. However, humility, self-doubt, and self-control are also essential.
- Leaders must be representative—yet not too representative; they need to consult and engage followers, and they need to respond to them. Yet they also must educate, motivate, and unlock the best in everyone.
- Leaders must be visionaries guided by ideas, ideals, and principles, yet we also want pragmatic realists guided by logic, facts, evidence, and level-headed rational analysis.
- Leaders reinvent themselves. Their leadership must be calculated, not accidental. Yet people also want their leaders to be open, relaxed, natural, sincere, spontaneous, and to somehow emerge from within rather than be imposed on a group.

- Leadership often calls for intensity, enthusiasm, passion, dramatization, and self-promotion—yet too much highly personalized volcanic energy can paralyze an organization. Too much of the *cult of personality* can create dependency or other organizational dysfunctions.
- Leaders need to unify their organizations or communities through effective negotiation and alliance building, yet leaders also have to stir things up and jolt their organizations out of complacency; be uniters *and* dividers.
- Leaders are supposed to lead, not follow the polls, yet they are often followers as much as they are leaders. One of the grand paradoxes of leadership is that leaders often follow, and followers often point the way and lead more than is appreciated. Change often comes from the bottom up rather than the top down. And it very often comes from the young, rather than establishment elites.
- Although we may reject the General George Patton or Godfather models of leadership for most of our organizations most of the time, we still want to believe leaders make a significant difference—yet idealistic and romantic theories exaggerate the impact of leaders. Most of the time, leaders are agents of their organizations or at least shaped by them more than they are agents of change.[33]

☐ Leaders as Introverts and Extroverts

As mentioned, leaders self-select. That is, they offer themselves up in hopes that others will follow. We often assume that leadership is the province of extroverts, those who are engaging, people-oriented, outgoing, and gregarious. Extroverts are energized when in the company of others. A crowd perks them up. They are, some believe, naturals for leadership positions.

Introverts, on the other hand, are people who find a great deal of human interaction a bit draining. They are comfortable when alone; in fact, alone-time is restoration. We might not expect such people to engage in the people-oriented world of politics and leadership. But such assumptions are misleading and often wrong. Many leaders are introverts, and introverts have many qualities that make them effective leaders (see Figure 1.2).

Roughly 25 to 30 percent of the population are introverts. Yet, an estimated 40 percent of all leadership positions are occupied by introverts (see Table 1.2). How can this be? It sounds so very counterintuitive.[34]

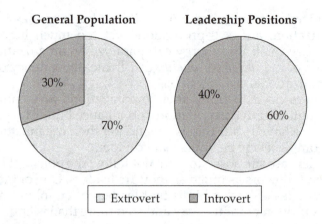

FIGURE 1.2   Introverts/Extroverts in the Population and in Leadership Positions

TABLE 1.2   Typical Characteristics*

Extroverts	Introverts
Energized by and seek out people; batteries "charged up" by other people	Energized by time alone; need time to "recharge" their batteries after interactions with other people
Talk first, think later	Think first, talk later
Talk out their thoughts	Process thoughts in their head
Enthusiastic	Reserved
Are transparent, easy to read—like a fur coat with the fur on the outside	Less demonstrative emotion in facial expressions—like a fur coat with the fur on the inside
Freely share personal data with friends and strangers	Share personal data with a select few
Prefer talking to writing	Prefer writing to talking
Focus on breadth	Focus on depth

* Jennifer B. Kahnweiler, *The Introverted Leaders: Building on Your Quiet Strength* (San Francisco, CA: Berrett-Koehler Publishers, 2009), p. 2.

Warren Buffett and Bill Gates are introverts. So are Abraham Lincoln, Mitt Romney, and Barack Obama. So too are Mother Teresa, Martin Luther King, Jr., Alfred Hitchcock, Michael Jordan, Thomas Edison, Clint Eastwood, Steve Martin (yes, that "wild and crazy guy"), Harrison Ford, and your author.

Some of our finest leaders have been introverts. In general, introverts are more cautious, more deliberate, tend to think through problems more carefully, examine options more thoroughly; in short, they are better decision makers.[35]

Another related distinction is found between those who are "insiders" and those who are "outsiders." Although the common expectation is that the leader will be a popular people-person extrovert, the reality is that many leaders are analytical or introverts, and many "change-leaders" are outsiders, rebels, marginal people who spend more of their time outside the mainstream: introverts such as Gandhi, King, Mandela, Steve Jobs, Thomas Paine, Camus and other outsiders may have changed the world more than all the outgoing people-persons combined.

What do these outsiders have that most insiders lack? They stood outside the mainstream, apart. They were not captured by the status quo, but rebelled against it.[36] Such rebellion may be a symptom of arrested adolescence, yet when the fire of politics burns, it can lead to transformational change. These outsiders may be less well suited in normal times, and yet how sad—and unjust—would the world be had not the Gandhis, Kings, and Mandelas not demanded change?

Almost everyone believes that leadership is necessary. Some see it as a positive good, others as a necessary evil, some as just plain evil, still others as a combination of all three. Although the need for leadership may be clear, measuring the "value added" of leadership rests on judgments, preference, ideology, and at times, who gets what. There is no leadership for all seasons, and there is no agreed upon way to evaluate or measure leadership effectiveness. It has something to do with power, purpose, interests, and achievement, and yet all those categories are contested territories. Leader X's achievements might be—to you—a measure of his or her greatness. To me, Leader X might efficiently be leading the nation over a cliff. It is one thing to know how to drive a bus, yet another thing to know *where* to take that bus.

Introverts tend to be more thoughtful and more risk-averse, and introverts study and reflect more deeply, and think things through more thoroughly.[37] Two classic extroverts, Bill Clinton and George W. Bush exhibit some of the key dangers of that personality type: Clinton in his reckless personal behavior that culminated in his impeachment, and Bush with his rush to war in Iraq without doing his due diligence.

Americans like our presidents to ooze confidence and hope for our collective future. We want to believe that tomorrow we will see better days. And those candidates who can articulate an optimistic, positive message usually win in presidential elections. Remember

Ronald Reagan's "America's best days are ahead of us" and compare that with Jimmy Carter's "turn down your thermostats," and you can see the power that positive thinking has over the electorate. In 2008, candidate Barack Obama sold "hope" to the American public when his opponent sold cranky. Hope wins.

It is understandable that we want to believe in a better tomorrow—it's all we have. But is it good for us? Is being drawn to the candidate who is confident, outgoing, extroverted, and optimistic healthy for the republic? Not always.

Research on decision making and from the emerging field on neuroscience warns us that leaders who are confident, outgoing, and optimistic often prove the most dangerous in office. And those leaders who are introverts, or slightly depressed, more often make better, more rational decisions. Although it may seem illogical, history, as well as research, bears this out.

Extroverts capture our imaginations, sometimes our hearts. We like and feel comfortable when our leaders are "people-persons," who evidently like themselves and others. We are comforted when they show confidence and optimism. By contrast, we have a hard time warming up to leaders who can't warm up to us. Introverts Romney and Obama had this problem in the 2012 election. Introverts seem aloof, even arrogant. Those who are depressed may suck the air out of any room—or nation—they occupy. We are uncomfortable with people like this, and they seem uncomfortable with us.

But let us not allow our hearts to get too far in front of our heads. The research on this is unmistakably clear: Happy people often do not make good decisions. Happy people are prone to be overconfident in their ability to control situations. Happy people often rush to judgment when a more thoughtful, measured response is required. Happy people tend to leap to conclusions and do not take the time or mental energy to consider the hard, tough choices. Happy people are also more prone to take unnecessary risk based on a presupposition that "everything will just work out."

Introverts, by contrast, are more likely to problem solve in a more direct and logical manner, employ suitable due diligence, think more thoroughly, explore more options, usually with an eye on the potential outcomes. Introverts and those who are slightly depressed often visualize a worst-case outcome, and take the time and effort needed to explore, examine, and try to identify the weak points in their arguments and the false chords in their assumptions. If you expect everything to "work out in the end," you will not devote yourself to the hard work of examination and self-examination. If you expect that things might fall apart, you are more careful and reasoned in your problem solving.

Exhibit A is Abraham Lincoln. Historians have long noted that Lincoln suffered from deep and repeated bouts of "melancholy." As a young man, he repeatedly and openly spoke of committing suicide. Similarly, Winston Churchill was plagued by a depression he called his "black dog" that followed him around. In Lincoln's case, we see how his depression and introverted nature led him to great pain over decisions, yet he was not paralyzed by his suffering. He was in fact ennobled by it. He converted his pain into empathy and understanding, and, being a deeper person, he was able to be a deeper thinker and a more capable decision maker.

Yes, I know, Richard Nixon was a depressed introvert.

Depression and introversion, rather than being impediments to leadership, usually make one a more capable leader and decision maker. Optimistic leaders like John F. Kennedy could be high risk takers as witnessed in both the Bay of Pigs decision (a disaster) and the Cuban Missile Crisis decision (a success). George W. Bush, strutting and playing the overconfident cowboy, with far too little thought or planning, embroiled the United States in the disaster of Iraq.

The introvert/extrovert distinction is not an either-or equation but should be seen as a continuum, with one *extreme* being introvert and the other extrovert. The ideal is perhaps a midpoint person, an *ambivert* who can more flexibly move from one point to the other as situations demand (see Figure 1.3).

As we face another choice of who shall have his hand on the wheel of history, we should keep in mind that often, what it takes to become president (optimism, confidence, self-assurance) is at odds with what is necessary to be an effective president. President Obama is more the introvert than extrovert. This got him into political hot water when he ended up taking so much time to decide what to do about U.S. involvement in Afghanistan. Critics accused him of being weak, vacillating, not being strong. Former President Bill Clinton once remarked, "Americans would rather have a president who is strong and wrong than weak and right." But in the case of Obama, being thoughtful, examining a variety of options,

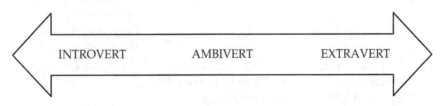

FIGURE 1.3 Dimensions of the Introvert/Extrovert Continuum

thinking deeply was the right thing to do, even if it was not the most politically advantageous course.

And so, let us celebrate the depressed introverts among us. They may be our only hope in these troubled times.

☐ Leadership and the Gender Questions

Do men and women lead differently? Early studies of the impact of gender on leadership—mostly done in large corporations—suggested that indeed there was a "male" and a "female" style of leadership.

The male style (X) tended to be hierarchical, command oriented, and about position and power. The female style (Y) was softer, more horizontal, more relationship and consensus-oriented, and more empathetic and collegial. These X and Y styles are now generally seen as caricatures. In fact, we now know that there is no one style of leadership that fits all seasons.[38] There are times when style X may be most useful, and other times that style Y is most appropriate. The key is not to be wedded to one narrow style but to be able to *style-flex*, that is, fit your style to the demands of the situation. This has led to the development of a third style (Z), which is the androgynous style of leadership (see Table 1.3).

TABLE 1.3 Gender and Leadership Dimensions

X	Z	Y
Male	**Androgynous**	**Female**
Hard	Flexible	Soft
Command-Oriented	Situation Driven	Collegial
Power	Context-Oriented	Cooperative
Hierarchical	Adaptive	Empathetic
Domination		Nurturing
		Empowering
		Partnership
		Influence
e.g., Generals Patton and MacArthur; George W. Bush; Margaret Thatcher	e.g., Abraham Lincoln; Franklin D. Roosevelt; Barack Obama	e.g., Corazon Aquino; Jimmy Carter

Effective leaders diagnose the situation and apply the appropriate style of leadership to the context: They fit their dance to the music. In battle, style X may be most useful. In developing education reform, style Y may be most appropriate.

The effective leader, the polymath leader, is a gender-bender who is capable of spanning the entire range of leadership styles. True, for centuries a more male-oriented style may have seemed most useful. After all, when the saber-toothed tiger threatened the family, physical strength—generally a male characteristic—was useful. In such a world, it should not surprise us that men dominated leadership positions. Once in command, they were understandably reluctant to give up control and promoted formal and informal standards to maintain power.

Today, physical strength is of little importance in leadership. In our transformed world, other qualities make for effective leadership. Today's leaders need to develop consensus, persuade, manage diversity, balance competing interest, arbitrate between competing demands, and manage group conflicts. These demands require more Y than X type leaders.

And yet, although we do not face saber-toothed tigers, we do face some very real threats. Thus, there will be time when an X type of leader is required. *That* is why the polymath leader of tomorrow must be androgynous, a Z type leader, capable of spanning all the wide range of leadership styles.

☐ Leadership and Sports

Until recently, boys participated in organized sports at a rate much higher than girls. Did this give boys a boost when they grew up and sought leadership positions?

Sports—at their best—teach teamwork, discipline, hard work, and leadership. Sports can be a useful analogy when trying to understand leadership as well, and one model of leadership is highly analogous to coaching.[39]

Good coaching and good leadership are quite similar. Hall of Fame quarterback Bart Starr, formally of the Green Bay Packers, recalls the team's first meeting with new coach Vince Lombardi. The Packers were 1–11 the previous season. Lombardi opened as follows, according to Starr:

> "He opened the session by thanking the Packers for allowing him to be their coach," Starr says. "That tells you something about the man." Then he quickly turned to us and said,

"Gentlemen, we are going to relentlessly chase perfection, knowing full well we will not catch it, because nothing is perfect. But we are going to relentlessly chase it, because in the process we will catch excellence." He came right up on us, within a foot of us in the front row, and then he said, "I am not remotely interested in just being good."[40]

The commitment to excellence proved contagious, and the Packers started one of football's greatest winning streaks, winning five NFL championships in seven seasons. Lombardi expected much, demanded excellence, insisted on teamwork and maximum effort, and inspired confidence in his players. His teams were hungry to win, determined, willing to let their egos serve a greater goal, unselfish, and of course, talented. He was a great coach, a successful coach, and a great leader.

There were other talented teams, other skilled coaches. What separated the Packers from others? Leadership and what George Plimpton calls "the X Factor." The Packers had both, as did the Chicago Bulls in the Jordan years, the Yankees of the Jeter era, and a few other teams. The X Factor is more than hard, disciplined practice—although greatness cannot be achieved without that. It is hard work, great coaching/teaching, skill, psychological strength and commitment, and the X Factor—a champion's attitude. The X Factor goes beyond natural gifts, beyond hard work, beyond good coaching, it is mental toughness mixed with the elusive X Factor. The X Factor—that added boost—can be seen in basketball stars Larry Bird and Michael Jordan, baseball great Derek Jeter, tennis greats Roger Federer and Jimmy Conners, and soccer star Pele.

Individuals have the X Factor; good coaches harness it and funnel it to team effort. George Plimpton, acknowledging the difficulty of clearly defining just what the X Factor is, attempting to explain it by listing the five chief characteristics that make it:

- Singleness of purpose
- Unselfishness
- Toughness
- Being smarter than your opponents
- Never quitting

Vince Lombardi could elicit this from his players, mold them into a team, prepare them for their opponent, inspire them, and then—step back. He empowered and prepared his players for excellence.

☐ What Power Does to the Leader

The exercise of leadership does something to the person who wields power.[41] As mentioned earlier, damaged people are often drawn to leadership because it promises being on stage or in the limelight, in addition to glamour, celebrity, status, power, and the possibility "to become someone special." It is often said that power corrupts. It does not. Power *reveals*. Often, people with power or celebrity status feel "entitled," feel they are owed special privileges, and exceptions. They may begin to expect more, demand special treatment, and insist on getting their own way. In the dysfunctional, power is certain to corrupt because it is tainted from the outset. All this reminds us of T. S. Eliot's line in *The Cocktail Party* that "half of the harm that is done in the world is due to the people who want to feel important."

"Man," playwright Eugene O'Neill reminds us, "is born broken," a disturbing yet important insight. This is especially important when we examine the role leaders play in the lives of citizens. When is leadership most likely to degenerate into dysfunctional behavior? There are several ways leadership becomes dysfunctional: (1) when ends justify the means; (2) when ideology becomes more important than anything else; and (3) when greed, love of power, excessive narcissism, or psychoses are unrestrained.

Of course, history offers us no shortage of such leaders.[42] Ironically, good leadership seems to involve small doses of all three of the factors mentioned in the previous paragraph. To lead effectively, one must be focused on the end, the goal; and at times (Lincoln during the Civil War, for example), the means may be less than ideal or pure. Also, a set of shared beliefs can help motivate followers to get involved, help develop a consensus, and animate behavior; finally, all leaders—to be effective—must know how to harness and use power.

Although leadership is necessary, it is also potentially dangerous. Just as leaders can help us reach desired goals, they may also bring us to tragic ends. We must be vigilant not only about the means of leadership but about the ends as well. Because leaders require followers, toxic or lazy followers are often as much at fault as that of the demonic leaders we revile. Hitler *did* have a significant following, as did Stalin, Mao, Klan leaders, Joseph McCarthy, and other misguided, dysfunctional leaders. We cannot sit back and condemn them if we do not accept some responsibility ourselves. After all, we colluded in ways to allow, even encourage, the rise of these dysfunctional leaders. "You cannot have power for good without having power for evil too," writes George Bernard Shaw. "Even mother's milk nourishes murderers as well as heroes."[43]

☐ The Dark Side

We have all been at the mercy of dysfunctional leaders over the years. People with dysfunctional characters or psychological problems are drawn to power and its uses. Some people are attracted to leadership for the *right* reasons: to do good, to solve tough problems, to help others, to make a better world. Others are attracted to leadership for the *wrong* reasons: to compensate for lack of self-esteem, to dominate or punish others for their own inadequacies, to feel powerful and loved.

A perplexing question is: why do we follow tyrants, bullies, and thugs? Usually, the *predicate* for the rise of a *popular* tyrant is social upheaval or crisis. This sets up the opportunity for a tyrant to gain attention, credibility, and a following. And yet, during the Depression and World War II, rather than follow a tyrant, England turned to Churchill, and the United States followed FDR. So what else is required for a tyrant to take command?

Tyrants often appeal to mass prejudices; they offer a beleaguered public a convenient, easy scapegoat for their problems; they are sometimes charismatic and experts at self-dramatization; they simplify complex realities and offer simple solutions to society's problems. In an atmosphere of fear and uncertainty, they give us what we think we need, what psychologically seems satisfying, and they offer hope, albeit distorted hope, for the future. People sometimes desperately follow a tyrant in the hope of being saved.

Such leaders offer comfort, reassurance, and hope. They promise a better future, however distorted their means for attaining it may be. Their certainty gives us something secure to grab hold of amid confusion. They make us feel part of something. In exchange, we surrender our freedom and turn a blind eye to their barbarism.

Dysfunctional leaders often rely upon and exploit what Harvard scholar Howard Gardner calls "chronic followers"—people who hunger for and willingly follow authoritarian leaders.[44] Such followers give their loyalty to leaders who appear confident and strong. They find that following such a "strong" leader gives them a sense of place, purpose, and meaning. They identify with, live through, and derive meaning by following.

Thus, we cannot divorce the dark side of leadership from the dark side of followership. Leaders may be evil, yet many willingly follow. Although we wish to believe that, "It can't happen here," we need only remember mass hysteria and blind followership of the anti-Communist witch hunts of the post-World War II McCarthy era, the followers who went along with Huey Long or the KKK, or the hatred demonstrated by opponents of civil rights reforms.

Negative leaders seduce us because we may, on some level, want to be seduced by, want to give ourselves to, want to "fall in love" with the leader. One person—usually a man—presents himself, offers himself, seduces us. And occasionally we do fall. We give ourselves to the cult of leadership as we submit to a lover. And we are often blinded by this love.

We may want our leaders to be pure, but ambitious; sometimes even ruthless ambition is necessary to, in the words of the great British Prime Minister Benjamin Disraeli, climb "to the top of the greasy pole." Thus, hunger, ambition, and drive are prerequisites of leadership; yet too much ambition corrupts.

☐ Portrait of a Polymath Leader

Thomas Jefferson: At an April 29, 1962, White House dinner honoring the Nobel Prize winners of the Western Hemisphere, President John Kennedy rose to give the toast, and said, "I want to tell you how welcome you are to the White House. I think this is the most extraordinary collection of talent, of human knowledge, that has ever been gathered together at the White House, with the possible exception of when Thomas Jefferson dined alone." High praise indeed. But praise most deserving, as Thomas Jefferson is considered one of the truly great men not only of his age, but of the ages.

A polymath leader familiar to our readers is Thomas Jefferson (1743–1826). Not only did Jefferson have an illustrious political career, serving as governor of Virginia, ambassador to France, U.S. secretary of state, vice president, and president, but he was also the primary author of the Declaration of Independence, wrote *Notes on the State of Virginia,* edited a volume on the teachings of Jesus, wrote the Virginia Statue for Religious Freedom, and cofounded a political party that still exists today (the Democratic Party).

Not content with an amazing political career, Jefferson also founded the University of Virginia, was an agriculturalist, anthropologist, architect, astronomer, bibliophile, botanist, classicist, ethnologist, farmer, geographer, gourmet, horseman, horticulturist, inventor, lawyer, lexicographer, linguist, mathematician, meteorologist, naturalist, numismatist, paleontologist, political philosopher, scientist, violinist, and writer. Jefferson was also fluent in Greek, Latin, French, Spanish, Italian, and German!

As the nation's third president, Jefferson allowed the Alien and Sedition Acts to expire, successfully prosecuted a war with the Barbary States over pirating, purchased the Louisiana territory from France for $15 million, thereby doubling the size of the United States and removing a potential rival from our borders, and authorized the Lewis and Clark Expedition. In historical rankings of U.S. presidents, Jefferson is usually rated as the fourth of fifth greatest presidents in history.[45]

Was the fact that Jefferson was a polymath the cause of his greatness, or merely an interesting historical fact? Causality is always difficult to ascertain, and success—like failure—has many fathers. Other men who were not polymaths were successful presidents, but Jefferson achieved greatness or notoriety, not just as president, but in many other fields as well. Had he only authored the Declaration of Independence he would have been famous. Yet not content to rest on his laurels, Jefferson piled invention on invention and success on success. Jefferson was not only a great president, he was also a great renaissance man. His greatness spanned many fields, as he did what great polymaths do: He connected the dots. He *saw* and *made* connections *across fields*. This is the main source of his creativity and success. Polymaths have the intellectual tools to cross borders. Great polymaths—like Jefferson—also have the skill to succeed at making these connections across fields.

☐ Notes

1. Max Weber, "Politics as a Vocation," speech delivered at Munich University in 1918; published by Duncker and Humboldt in Munich, 1919.
2. Samuel Beckett, *Waiting for Godot*; play premiered at the *Theater de Babylone*, Paris, July 5, 1953.
3. See Bruce J. Avolio, *Leadership Development in Balance: MADE/Born* (Mahwah, NJ: Lawrence Erlbaum, 2004).
4. Thomas E. Cronin and Michael A. Genovese, *Leadership Matters: Unleashing the Power of Paradox* (Boulder, CO: Paradigm Publishers, 2012), pp. vii–viii.
5. Robert Michels, *Political Parties: A Sociological Study of the Oligarchical Tendencies of Modern Democracy* (New York, NY: Free Press, 1915).
6. Michael Harvey, "Leadership and the Human Condition," in *The Quest for a General Theory of Leadership*, ed. George R. Goethals and Georgia L. J. Sorenson (Chetterhand, England: Edward Elgar, 2006), pp. 39–40.
7. *The American Heritage Dictionary* (Boston, MA: Houghton Mifflin, 1991).

8. Crispin Burke, "T. E. Lawrence: A Leadership Vignette for a Successful Counter-Insurgent," *Small Wars Journal*, posted by SLOJ Editors (February 19, 2009): www.smallwarsjournal.com.
9. January 9, 1961, speech before the Massachusetts Legislature, Boston.
10. Thomas Carlyle, "On Heroes, Hero-worship and the Heroic in History," ed. Carl Niemeyer (Lincoln, NE: University of Nebraska Press, 1966 [originally published in 1841]).
11. Quoted in Norman W. Provizer, "Two Trains Running: Tolstoy on Lincoln and Leadership," in *Leadership: Impact, Culture, and Sustainability,* ed. Nancy S. Huber and Michael Harvey (College Park, MD: International Leadership Association, 2007).
12. See Tolstoy's epilogue to *War and Peace*, where he writes that "The life of nations is not contained in the life of a few men."
13. Robert Tucker, *Politics and Leadership* (Columbia, MO: University of Missouri Press, 1995), p. 27.
14. Steven Sample, *The Contrarian's Guide to Leadership* (San Francisco, CA: Jossey-Boss, 2003), pp. 191–192.
15. James MacGregor Burns, *Transforming Leadership* (New York, NY: Atlantic Monthly Press, 2003), pp. 14–15.
16. Provizer, "Two Trains Running: Tolstoy on Lincoln and Leadership," p. 22.
17. Alexis de Tocqueville, *Democracy in America*, ed. J. P. Mayer (New York, NY: Perennial Library, 1988), p. 705. Two volumes, originally published in 1835 and 1840.
18. Quoted in Burns, *Transforming Leadership*, p. 15.
19. See Barbara Tuchman, *The March of Folly: From Troy to Vietnam* (New York, NY: Ballantine Books, 1985).
20. See, for example, J. G. Randall and Richard N. Currant, *Lincoln the President*, Vol. 2 (New York, NY: Da Capo Press, 1997); and Daniel Farber, *Lincoln's Constitution* (Chicago, IL: The University of Chicago Press, 2003).
21. Dean Keith Simonton, *Genius, Creativity, and Leadership* (Cambridge, MA: Harvard University Press, 1984), pp. 152–155.
22. Laurence C. Smith, *The World in 2050* (New York, NY: Dutton, 2010); Edward Cornish, *Futuring: The Exploration of the Future* (Bethesda, MD: World Future Society, 2004); Richard Watson, *Future File* (London, England: Nicholas Brealey Publishing, 2010); and Al Gore, *The Future: Six Drivers of Global Change* (New York, NY: Random House, 2013).
23. See Anne-Marie Slaughter, "Problems Will Be Global—And Solutions Will Be, Too," *Foreign Policy* (September/October 2011): p. 89.
24. Moises Naim, *The End of Power* (New York, NY: Basic Books, 2013).
25. Angel Cabrera and Gregory Unruh, *Being Global* (Boston, MA: Harvard Business Review Press, 2012); Adrian Done, *Global Trends* (New York, NY: Palgrave Macmillan, 2012); Howard Gardner, *5 Minds for the Future* (Boston, MA: Harvard Business Press, 2008); and Daniel H. Pink, *A Whole New Mind* (New York, NY: Riverhead, 2005).

26. Jeff Faux, "Whose Rules for Globalization?," *The American Prospect* 5 (June 2001); and Wayne Ellwood, *The No-Nonsense Guide to Globalization* (London, England: Verso, 2001).
27. Schumpeter, "In Praise of Misfits," *The Economist* (June 2, 2012).
28. See Cronin and Genovese, *Leadership Matters*, pp. 291–293.
29. For a way to reconcile corporate capitalism with the demands of the future, see John Mackey and Raj Sisodia, *Conscious Capitalism: Liberating the Heroic Spirit of Business* (Boston, MA: Harvard Business Review Press, 2013).
30. Carne Ross, *The Leaderless Revolution: How Ordinary People Will Take Power and Change Politics in the 21st Century* (New York, NY: Plume, 2011); and Moises Naim, *The End of Power: From Boardrooms to Battlefields and Churches to States, Why Being in Charge Isn't What It Used to Be* (New York, NY: Basic Books, 2013).
31. See Daniel Goleman, *The Brain and Emotional Intelligence* (Northampton, MA: More than Sound, 2011), p. 41.
32. For an excellent short analysis of power, see Robert Caro, *The Power Broker: Robert Moses and the Fall of New York* (New York, NY: Vintage Books, 1975), introduction.
33. Cronin and Genovese, *Leadership Matters*, pp. 3–4.
34. See Jennifer B. Kahnweiler, "Why Introverts Can Make the Best Leaders," *Forbes Magazine* (November 30, 2009).
35. See Bryan Walsh, "The Upside of Being an Introvert (And Why Extroverts Are Overrated)," *TIME* (February 6, 2012).
36. In the movie *The Wild One,* the Marlon Brando rebel character is asked, "What are you rebelling against?," to which he replies, "What'd ya got?" See also the 1965 S. E. Hinton book, *The Outsiders,* made into a movie in 1983.
37. Susan Cain, *Quiet: The Power of Introverts in a World That Can't Stop Talking* (New York, NY: Crown, 2012); Marti Olson Land, *The Introvert Advantage: How To Thrive in an Extrovert World* (New York, NY: Workman Publishing, 2002); Laurie Helgoe, *Introvert Power: Why Your Inner Life Is Your Hidden Strength* (Naperville, IL: Sourcebooks, 2008); and Jennifer B. Kahnweiler, *The Introverted Leader: Building on Your Own Quiet Strength* (San Francisco, CA: Barrett Koehler, 2009).
38. Michael A. Genovese and Janie Steckenrider, eds., *Women as Political Leaders* (New York, NY: Routledge, 2013).
39. See Bill Dwyer, "A Man of Integrity," *Los Angeles Times Magazine* (March 29, 1995; on John Wooden); David Shields, "The Good Father," *New York Times Magazine* (April 23, 2000; on Phil Jackson); and Michael Sokolove, "Happiness Is a Warm Football Coach," *New York Times Magazine* (November 2008; on USC football coach Peter Carrell).
40. Jeremy Schapp, "We Will Catch Excellence," *Parade Magazine* (February 3, 2008): p. 8.
41. Xandra Kayden, *Surviving Power: The Experience of Power—Exercising It and Giving It Up* (New York, NY: The Free Press, 1990).
42. See H. E. Barnes, *The Story of Punishment: A Record of Man's Inhumanity to Man,* 2nd rev. ed. (Glen Ridge, NJ: Patterson Smith, 1996); and

Benjamin Valentino, *Final Solutions: Mass Killings and Genocide in the Twentieth Century* (Ithaca, NY: Cornell University Press, 2004).

43. George Bernard Shaw, *Major Barbara* (New York, NY: Penguin Books, 1968). See also, the distinction about different types of evil and what our responses should be in Alan Wolfe, *Political Evil* (New York, NY: Knopf, 2011).

44. Howard Gardner, *Leading Minds: An Anatomy of Leadership* (New York, NY: Basic Books, 1996), p. 35.

45. See Robert M. Johnstone, Jr., *Jefferson and the Presidency, Leadership in the Young Republic* (Ithaca, NY: Cornell University Press, 1978). Dumas Malone, *Jefferson and the Ordeal of Liberty* (Boston, MA: Little, Brown, 1962); *Jefferson the President: First Term, 1801–1805* (Boston, MA: Little, Brown, 1970); *Jefferson the President: Second Term, 1805–1809* (Boston, MA: Little, Brown, 1974); and *Thomas Jefferson as a Political Leader* (Berkeley, CA: University of California Press, 1963). Willard S. Randall, *Thomas Jefferson: A Life* (New York, NY: Holt, 1993); Robert W. Tucker, *Empire of Liberty: The Statecraft of Thomas Jefferson* (New York, NY: Oxford University Press, 1990).

A Leadership Composite from the Classics

"Start by doing what is necessary, then what is possible, and suddenly you are doing the impossible."

—St. Francis of Assisi

Genovese Leadership Theorem: The unexamined life is not worth living, and the examined life can be hard on us.

Let's ask the world's deepest thinkers on leadership, just what skills, attributes, traits, or temperaments are needed to be an effective ruler. Can we draw up a composite portrait of what the great classical thinkers view as the *ideal type* of leader? Here, we turn for advice to the Greeks, Plato and Aristotle; one Italian, Niccolo Machiavelli; and one Englishman, William Shakespeare, for help and guidance.

Plato: A student of Socrates, Plato (429–347 BCE) founded the Academy in Athens, considered the first academy of higher education in the West. Plato's Athens was a participatory democracy. No fan of democracy himself, Plato believed that only highly trained individuals should govern.

The Republic was written shortly after the Peloponnesian War (from 431–404 BCE) when Athens faced troubling times. Its democracy sometimes descended into chaos and anarchy, with the occasional despot emerging to impose a temporary tyranny. Plato believed that democracies lead to tyranny as the masses were prone to "honor as a good and profoundly wise person any obsequious flatterer" and were "bound to disapprove of all who pursue wisdom."

Plato's *philosopher-king* was to be good morally (to know justice) and good as a leader (to act justly). Only a man deeply trained in philosophy and other high arts was capable of both knowing justice (a philosopher) and acting efficiently to bring justice about (a king).

Plato saw the masses becoming a mob, prone to inflamed passions and irrational exuberance. To please the people, not necessarily do what was right, was the goal of the leaders in Athenian democracy. Plato saw little room for true statesmanship in a world where politicians were required to feed the appetites of the masses.

His disdain for democracy drove Plato to offer a competing paradigm, found in Book V of *The Republic*. Plato had a specific vision for effective leadership: a philosopher-king. As Plato wrote,

> Until philosophers are kings, or the kings and princes of this world have the spirit and power of philosophy, and political greatness and wisdom meet in one, and those commoner natures who pursue either to the exclusion of the other are compelled to stand aside, cities will never have rest from their evils,—no, nor the human race, as I believe,—and then only will this our State have a possibility of life and behold the light of day.

Plato feared leadership by amateurs. He saw leadership as a specialized skill that could be learned. And, it took a lifetime devoted to learning this craft. Leadership is a specialized knowledge, and Plato demonstrated this by way of a metaphor:

> The sailors are quarrelling over the control of the helm . . . They do not understand that the genuine navigator can only make himself fit to command a ship by studying the seasons of the year, sky, stars, and winds, and all that belongs to his craft; and they have no idea that, along with the science of navigation, it is possible to gain, by instruction or practice, the skill to keep control of the helm whether some of them like it or not. If a ship were managed in that way, would not those on board be likely to call the expert in navigation a mere stargazer, who spent his time in idle talk and was useless to them?

Should the most popular become the leader? The most handsome? The most athletic? The greatest warrior? The smartest? No, only the person trained in the art and science of leadership—only the most qualified to perform the task—should lead.

And only a philosopher-king is qualified to govern. As all men are susceptible to excess and corruption, what distinguishes Plato's philosopher-king from others? His ruler can enjoy neither private property nor the joys of family life. The philosopher-king studies philosophy, knows justice, and acts justly. He is *trained* for years in the arts of leadership. The philosopher-king studies math, geometry, and dialectics; he must do extensive public service in military and administrative capacities; he must take up the life of the philosopher, then he may eventually govern the polity. The key components of Plato's leadership are summed up as:

- Leadership is an individualized activity.
- As long as the ruler is concerned with the common good, citizens are expected to follow.
- A benevolent tyrant is preferable to rule by the masses.
- Only after extensive specialized training might one be qualified to lead.
- The leader's job is not to please the people but to do the right thing.
- Only a philosopher could lead justly.[1]

Plato describes both the potential dangers of democratic leadership and the specialized training and temperament essential to govern effectively.

In a democracy, leaders would likely pander to the masses. And yet, in Plato's *Republic*, we are still left with one of the most fundamental questions of leadership, asked by the Roman poet and critic Juvenal: "who shall guard the guardians?"

Plato insists that leaders need expert knowledge that can be attained only through years of rigorous training and education. Plato, as well as others who study modern leadership, insist that, leadership can be taught. But is good *judgment* more important than good *training*? Are common sense, a curious nature, intelligence, a natural skepticism, a hunger for knowledge, a good evaluation of talent, and a sense of timing more important that specialized training? Can common sense be taught? Judgment? Leaders need a variety of personal skills and a robust emotional and contextual intelligence as well as training and experience. Plato's insistence on a specific type of benevolent dictatorship of the philosophically trained may have superficial appeal, yet falls short when it meets the harsh reality of politics in practice.

The ideal leader exercises *prudence*, exhibits *courage* and *temperance*, and knows as well as works for *justice*.[2] Would a democracy elect such a person? No. Only concerted training would produce a leader with such virtues. Leaders *are* special; they must have *special training*; therefore, leadership *can be taught.*

Plato's philosopher-king is a repudiation of the Athenian democracy of his age, and of popular government in general. His leader is a self-consciously elitist king, trained in the art and science of governing. Citizens were untrained in the skills required to govern effectively. Only expert knowledge—a recognition that governing required special skills that could be learned—could guide the state in the right direction.

Plato, and Socrates before him, enjoined leader and citizen to "know thyself." They insisted that "the unexamined life is not worth living." Sound advice for leaders then; sound advice for leaders today.

Plato's mentor Socrates gave us one of the most important clues for leadership success: asking the right questions. An effective leader does not have all of the answers, and further, the leader *knows* he or she does not have all the answers. But a smart person and a smart leader is curious, open, willing to recognize and admit fallibility, *and* keeps on probing, questioning, and asking the questions.

Aristotle: A student of Plato's, Aristotle (384–322 BCE), nonetheless, broke with his mentor and developed his own approach to philosophy and leadership. In his *Politics,* he categorizes governments as falling into one of three different regimes or types: *monarchy* (rule by the one, sometimes referred to as kingship); *oligarchy* (rule by the few); and *democracy* (rule by the many). Each regime is susceptible to the dangers inherent in their natures. Monarchies often degenerate into *tyranny*; an oligarchy can become an *aristocracy*, and democracy can slip into *anarchy*. To Aristotle, the government with the best chance of surviving and thriving was a *mixed regime,* a kind of separation of powers or checks and balances system that combines elements of each regime but stresses the oligarchic and democratic forms.

Although it is a great disservice to reduce Aristotle's views down to a few key points, we can focus on his views on leadership to discern some of his thoughts on what constituted good leadership.[3] Aristotle sought *the golden mean,* a type of prudent pursuit of self and community interests. Humans were both individual and political (community-oriented) animals. Individuals, through the practice of good acts, developed good (persistent) habits. This applied to both individual behaviors and toward communal goals and acts.

True happiness and harmony were reached when each individual found his or her intended purpose, and developed his or her skill to the fullest. This was the pursuit of virtue and excellence. We do not pursue virtue and excellence merely for self-gain, however.

Because we are also political animals, we need communion in civil society. In short, we need others. Our fulfillment takes place not in isolation but in the good individual life *and* the good community. What role does leadership play in this process? Aristotle sees the ideal leader as practicing what he called *phronesis*.

Aristotle rejected the dominant view of his time that cast the world in either/or terms (good versus bad), and developed a more nuanced approach that posited a *golden mean* or middle ground as the ideal. His goal of achieving balance struck some as too moderate, yet Aristotle saw this as a more realistic approach. After all, we are not pure saints or impure sinners. We are human, imperfect, yet capable of reason and growth. In a slap at his mentor Plato, he asserted that we cannot create perfect leaders nor perfect institutions, but we can become better. Human nature makes us prone to mistakes; reason offers some prospect for improvement. No utopian, Aristotle offers us a difficult path that promises little yet offers a modicum of hope.

His major works *Politics* and *Nicomachean Ethics* use empirical observation as a starting point, and then build his philosophy around the belief that the essential characteristic of human beings is our ability to reason. More advanced humans develop their reasoning abilities and thus have a greater chance to attain happiness as we search for the good life.

Life is about the journey, or the process of seeking higher forms of fulfillment and rationality as we attempt to find and achieve the elusive good life.[4] The end result—happiness—comes from contemplation on higher order values and living a life in accordance with those virtues that help maximize our potential to achieve *Eudiamonia* (needs rooted in human nature that lead to growth). Growth toward our best selves leads to happiness. It is self-actualization, a learned process of development toward a morally sound goal, or toward the pursuit of excellence. This pursuit to Aristotle involves both individual development and engagement in the affairs of one's community. The highest form of excellence is to attain happiness, then create conditions for others to grow and develop—that is leadership.

The leader who achieved excellence, then paved the way for others to engage in that pursuit, gave to the community, helped it achieve its potential, and enriched and empowered others. Good leaders are both effective *and* virtuous.

Aristotle's goal to help guide the enlightened statesperson toward effective leadership and stewardship is best seen in his discussion of phronesis. Phronesis means knowledge translated into appropriate action for a good or morally worthy cause. It is reason and sound judgment, logic as applied to a complex world, recognizing the limits and possibilities at hand, and deciding on a constructive course of action that is most likely to lead to a morally and politically good result. The verb phronein means "intelligent awareness," and the noun phronesis means "practical prudence, or sound deliberation resulting in correct suppositions about a good end." Wisdom, prudence, good judgment, right action, morally appropriate ends—these are the factors that bring *phronesis* to life. It is moral discernment applied to human affairs, prudence in action, goal maximization designed to achieve socially good ends, and it is what defines good leadership.

Phronesis is more than mere prudence, it is prudent judgment directed into action designed to achieve a good result. It is *judgment* and *action*. In this way, phronesis is an explicit recognition of both the moral and pragmatic dimensions of effective action. The leader who possesses the skills to govern effectively has competence, judgment, and a sense of proportion and justice. This person has the necessary skills to govern effectively and the ethical compass to govern wisely.

Niccolo Machiavelli: Niccolo Machiavelli (1469–1527), Florentine diplomat turned philosopher, has, to put it mildly, a bad reputation. The name alone sends shivers down the spine. To be called a Machiavellian is to be referred to as manipulative and underhanded, someone in league with the devil. Today, over five hundred years after his death, he still evokes images of cunning and evil, an amalgam of a Mao, the Godfather, and the Lord Voldemort.

Bertrand Russell called *The Prince* (1513) "a handbook for gangsters"; the Catholic Church placed both *The Prince* and *The Discourses* on its index of banned books, the *Index Librorum Prohitorum*.

Yet if Machiavelli's *The Prince* was publicly condemned, it was widely read. Cardinal Richelieu read it several times; Napoleon consulted it often; President John Adams kept a copy at his bedside. Voltaire helped the Prussian king Frederick the Great write a broadside against *The Prince* entitled *The Anti-Machiavel*. Frederick was, however, not at all shy about employing Machiavelli's methods—when thought to be useful. In short, virtually everyone read his work, from the founding fathers in America to modern corporate chiefs, to Adolph Hitler. It is certainly the most widely read book on leadership strategy and tactics in history.

Machiavelli's principle "crime" in *The Prince* was to defy convention and openly present a stark portrait of the naked use of power divorced from the Christian ethics so prominent in his time. *The Prince* was also an attack on the classical as well as the Christian tenants of political thought. Machiavelli argued that such high-minded advice, although sounding nice, was simply wrong, so he subverted the conventional wisdom. Before Machiavelli, Statecraft was deeply connected to soulcraft: A good man would make a good prince. Thus, from Plato's Philosopher King to Erasmus's Christian Prince, the ruler was taught to know justice and act justly. The teaching of virtue was to be the check and balance limiting the behavior of the prince. At least that was the hope.

Machiavelli thought this was a patently false premise. He divorced statecraft from soulcraft and focused on the former. Machiavelli was concerned with *how* leaders behaved, not how they *ought* to behave.

Realism was Machiavelli's goal. In advising the prince, he offered good advice rather than advice on how to be good. He had what might be called a jaundiced view of human nature, seeing ambition and the hunger for power as trumping personal morality. Machiavelli sought an understanding of how princes actually behaved, thereby affording him the opportunity to advise the prince in ways to gain and use power wisely in the real world.

Although many argue to the contrary, clearly his goal was not to justify evil. He merely described *how* leaders behaved. And in the sometimes brutal world of power politics, to survive, one had to know how the game was played, and what it took to win. At times, fighting fire with fire made political sense. Machiavelli did not advise the prince to do evil; he merely suggested that under certain conditions it might be necessary to do so. He argued that the prince must be able not to depart from good where possible, but to know how to enter into evil, when forced by necessity.

The Prince argues that three ingredients lead to success: *virtu, fortuna*, and *occasione*. By virtu he does not mean goodness, but ability, skill, intelligence, judgment, decisiveness, and a disciplined sense of power. Fortuna means fate, fortune, or luck. Some are blessed with good luck, others are not. Napoleon often said "find me a lucky general!" Occasione refers to opportunity and the proper reading of context or situation. When virtu, fortuna, and occasione were aligned, effective leadership was likely. Yet only virtu was under the control of the prince. When virtu and prudence (*prudenza*) and occasione could be artfully combined, the prince could maintain his power and serve the common good.

What are the chief components of individual virtu? The effective leader was capable of being (as each situation demanded) generous or cruel, faithless and compassionate, faithful and frivolous, affable and selfish, religious and unbelieving, caring and haughty, rapacious and miserly. In short, the effective leader could be many different things depending on what was needed at any particular time. Effective leaders were smart, flexible, and adaptable. He was able to style-flex, fitting his dance to the music being played. He could accurately diagnose the situation (occasione), and match his style of leadership to the needs of the situation (virtue), and if lucky (fortuna), perhaps emerge victorious. Yet for Machiavelli, even the right decision at the right time could lead to failure if fortuna did not favor the leader. Such are the vagaries of leadership in a complex world.

Machiavelli does not call for the exercise of cunning for its own sake. That would be dysfunctional. However, the occasional use of cunning may be necessary to preserve or advance power. It is only wise to use cunning when it is absolutely necessary.

The leader must be prepared to be good or not good as the situation demands. At times, the prince must play the fox who can recognize traps, whereas at other times, the prince must be the lion who can frighten wolves. As Machiavelli notes in Chapter XVIII:

> Everyone knows how praiseworthy it is for a ruler to keep his promises and live uprightly and not by trickery. Nevertheless, experience shows that in our times the rulers who have done great things are those who have set little store by keeping their word, being skillful rather in cunningly confusing men; they have got the better of those who have relied on being trustworthy.

Of course, Machiavelli did not invent the ideas that are associated with Machiavellianism. His ideas had been practiced by leaders for centuries. He did however, have the audacity to openly defy religious niceties and write about a stark and to some—harsh reality.

For Machiavelli, the best way to gain control was to acquire power through honorable means. This allowed one to have both power and glory. Yet in a harsh world, such high-mindedness is not always possible. Thus, the other way was to gain power by whatever means necessary. One acquired power, but not glory. Machiavelli directs the prince to use power wisely and well, brutally where necessary, and always to be conscious of his status. The skillful pursuit and use of power is Machiavelli's goal.

Yes, Machiavelli's prince seems more concerned with power than justice, something Plato, Aristotle, and the ancients would find objectionable, yet there is nothing in *The Prince* that argues against the promotion of justice. It is merely that to achieve a good end—and to Machiavelli, the good end ultimately sought was a unified, republican Italy—the prince must be in control and powerful. If Machiavelli does not explicitly link power to principle in *The Prince,* he does so more clearly in *The Discourses.* Also, Machiavelli does not ask for a moral escape clause for the leader. He does not argue that evil is not evil. He merely notes that if your adversary is using evil tactics, you would likely lose if you were to remain morally pure.

William Shakespeare: Arguably the world's greatest playwright, William Shakespeare (1546–1616) was also one of the most insightful students of human nature and human behavior in all its manifest forms. More than any other writer, Shakespeare lays before us the good, the bad, and the ugly of power and the precarious nature of the human condition. His insights into leadership and the use and abuse of power by tyrants and kings gives us instructive images of power and principle.[5]

Shakespeare enjoins us to reflect deeply on leadership. Shakespeare asks the perennial questions, explores the pressures and possibilities, confronts the good and bad in us and in leaders, and squarely exposes the dilemmas and paradoxes of authority, position, and leadership.

About twenty of his plays deal explicitly with power, politics, and leadership, especially his histories and tragedies. Leadership succession, rulership, the uses and abuses of power, manipulation and deceit, authority, power, ego and jealousy, and themes of the rule of law reverberate in his classic works.

Although we may never know with certainty what Shakespeare's political convictions were, we do know that Shakespeare wrote in an age of upheaval, when the doctrine of the divine right of kings was receding and demands for more representative and popular forms of government were rising in England and elsewhere.

In Shakespeare's time, most educated people believed in the legitimacy of a hierarchical order. This order was being challenged, and fears of approaching anarchy were very real. The Elizabethan doctrine of order and obedience to the king were still in vogue in Shakespeare's age, and to a degree, his plays reflect adherence to this principle. No democrat, the extent to which Shakespeare embraced a hierarchical model of society and politics, remains unclear.

Hierarchy, to Shakespeare, represented the true order of nature. And in his age, to live according to nature was to live in concert with God's will; and if the king ruled in the name of God, one had an obligation to obey God's earthly voice. As God ruled over us, so too must a king be God's temporal ruler on earth.

Although Shakespeare accepts the legitimacy of a hierarchical order, he is nonetheless concerned that the king rule justly and effectively. His good kings consult widely and are open and willing to accept and learn from criticism. Rulers who are arrogant and egotistic fail of their own weaknesses. Shakespeare did not question monarchy—he was, after all, a man of his age. But he did question the ruling strategies of many of the kings he examined. He does not give his monarchs a free pass. Tyranny is derided, and only good rulers meet Shakespeare's approval.[6]

Shakespeare's leading characters work within different regimes of power, and how each performs—the choices made—determine their own fortunes and also the fortunes of the state. Where their choices are intended for self promotion, they usually fail; when their choices are made rashly, they fail; when they decide based on poor or faulty information, they usually fail; where they are too self-absorbed, they fail. It is in choosing that Shakespeare's politics play out. Fate plays a role, but human intervention—choice—matters most. Therefore, leaders matter.

Shakespeare's suspicion of democracy is evident in both *Julius Caesar* and *Coriolanus*. He saw the common man as fickle, irrational, and prone to manipulation. People fell in love with Caesar and welcomed his autocratic rule; this invited tyranny. Equally weak is the foundation on which republican rule is built. And when the republic collapses, and Caesar is killed, a new brand of tyranny is unleashed—the tyranny of the mob.

Shakespeare valued order and believed order came in large part from good leadership. What to Shakespeare constituted good leadership? Shakespeare's focus on the importance of individual agency reinforces the conception not only that leadership matters, but that leaders are virtually all that matters. This leader-centric view helps shape public and elite opinion and supports the leader-as-hero (or sometimes villain) linage that dominates thinking even into our day. What constitutes good and bad leadership? Military leaders fare poorly in his world. Macbeth, Othello, Titus Andronicus, Henry Bolingbroke, and Coriolanus all appear as too quick to act, too cynical, hardened, and rash.

Shakespeare warns us that greed, ambition, and swollen egos figure prominently in human affairs, lead most often to failure, and are presented as dysfunctional and counterproductive. He did not question the legitimacy of the monarchy, but cautioned against overreaching. In attempting to define the ideal prince, Shakespeare would have been familiar with the works of Erasmus (*The Education of a Christian Prince*, 1603), as well as Machiavelli, and may in fact have modeled his good princes on Erasmus, whereas his villains display a certain Machiavellian wickedness even Machiavelli would have condemned. What makes Shakespeare's villains so deliciously attractive is their high level of self-awareness of their vulgar acts. Richard III turns to enlisting us in his self-justifications. Shakespeare's flawed characters take morality seriously, especially as they violate conventional morals in favor of self-serving expediency.

The stability of the state depends largely on the skill of the prince. As Rosencrantz reminds us in *Hamlet*:

> The single and peculiar life is bound
> With all the strength and armour of the mind
> To keep itself from noyance; but much more
> That spirit upon whole weal depends and rests
> The lives of many. The cease of majesty
> Dies not alone, but like a gulf doth draw
> What's near it with it. It is a massy wheel.
> Fix'd on the summit of the highest mount,
> To whole huge spokes ten thousand lesser things
> Are mortis'd and adjoin'd; which when it falls,
> Each small annexment, petty consequence,
> Attends the bois'trous ruin. Never alone
> Did the king sigh, but with a general groan.[7]

☐ Conclusion

So can we pan for leadership gold in the minds of great thinkers? Is there a composite great leadership ideal type that emerges from our cursory examination of the leadership insights from Plato, Aristotle, Machiavelli, and Shakespeare?

From Plato, we are reminded that leadership is a *specialized* skill that requires years of *training*. Amateurs need not apply. From Aristotle, we learn the importance of *phronesis*, the art of accurately reading the situation, devising a workable plan for moving toward a morally worthwhile goal, and employing skill to achieve that goal. From Machiavelli, we learn that to be effective, that leader must be concerned with his status and power, learn from the lessons of history, ground action in realism, be flexible, use good judgment, and do what is *necessary* to achieve a laudable goal. And from Shakespeare we learn to be sensitive to the vagaries of the human condition, the strengths and weakness inherent in each of us, the temptations and traps into which we so often fall, and not let our egos overwhelm our judgment.

Important lessons, all. Yet only a beginning. It remains for us to look more deeply at the skills necessary for good leadership.

☐ Notes

1. See Cronin and Genovese, *Leadership Matters*, pp. 82–84.
2. T. Takala, "Plato on Leadership," *Journal of Business Ethics 17* (1998): pp. 785–798.
3. James O'Toole, *Creating the Good Life* (Emmaus, PA: Rodale, 2005); Tom Morris, *If Aristotle Ran General Motors* (New York, NY: Holt Paperbacks, 1998).
4. Herman Hesse sees a similar path-oriented or journey-driven search for truth as the true meaning of life. See *Siddhartha* (Scotts Valley, CA: Createspace, 2008).
5. See Bruce Altschuler and Michael A. Genovese, *Shakespeare and Politics* (Boulder, CO: Paradigm Publishers, 2013).
6. See Allan Bloom and Henry V. Jaffa, *Shakespeare's Politics* (New York, NY: Basic Books, 1964); and Michael Platt, *Rome and Romans According to Shakespeare* (Lanham, MD: University Press of America, 1982).
7. *Hamlet*, Act III.

The Leadership Toolkit

"Anyone can hold the helm when the sea is calm."
—Publilius Syrus

Genovese Leadership Theorem: Curiosity didn't kill the cat, stupidity did.

☐ Key Leadership Competencies

A central premise of this book is that leadership can be learned. Anyone can become a *better* leader. But not everyone can become a Mount Rushmore type of leader. Improvement, yes; mastery, that is a more difficult task.

In order to become a better leader, what skills or competencies must be developed? What type of targeted training or purposeful, deliberative practice helps make one a more effective leader?

Leadership learning takes place at several stages during our lives. We are born with certain genes that may give us a leg up over others. But while genes may be our start-up point, over time nature gives way to nurture and we sometimes consciously, often unconsciously, begin to develop as leaders.

The first stage is the *accident of birth*. Although there is no leadership gene passed down from generation to generation, some of us are born with certain advantages or disadvantages. Some are born to the advantage of wealth, others must overcome poverty. If my goal is to play center for the Boston Celtics, it would help to be 6'11" rather than 5'11". Thus, the accident of birth may limit some of my options. In leadership terms, some are born with better genes that make leadership more likely. To be tall, have a strong speaking voice, to be attractive, etc. may add to my appeal as well as my skill base. But just as more is required if I am 6'11" and want to play basketball (I must work hard, be coordinated, train properly, eat right, etc.) so too must I take the genes with which I was born and do something with them. An early gene boost helps but is not sufficient. Hard work and skill development also matter.

The second stage involves *early childhood development*. We learn from the teachers, coaches, scout leaders, ministers, and most of all from parents who exhibit different styles of leadership. One baseball coach berates and humiliates us when we make an error; another is more supportive and encouraging. One minister breathes fire and brimstone; another offers a loving God. One teacher is open and generous; another is stern and demanding. We take away from these experiences certain lessons about ourselves and about leadership.

Also, early childhood traumas—losing a parent for example—can have a deep impact on how we view the world, ourselves, and our role in leading a family.

Today, expert coaching in various sports starts as early as eight years of age. Coaching is good, but as in all things, we can go too far. Making little Timmy into an obsessive-compulsive one-dimensional machine may lead to his development in one particular thing, yet stunts his growth in other areas and may warp his outlook on life.

"Intensive football training before puberty is not what your neighborhood neurologist has lately been recommending. Developing brains are elastic in more ways than one, and especially susceptible to the long-term effects of bouncing around inside a skull."[1]

In this, as in all things, let us follow the master, Aristotle who cautions us to find balance or the golden mean.[2]

The third stage, the *journey to maturity* offers other leadership lessons for us. In school, on sports teams, in clubs, and elsewhere, some emerge (self or peer-selected) as formal or informal leaders. Team captains, class presidents, debating teams, and other activities foster leadership growth. Later in life, more formal training in leadership skills can have a significant impact. A military academy, business school, the Young Presidents Organization, the Junior League, and volunteer organizations are some of the *developmental leagues* that prepare us to become leaders.

The final stage consists of our *experience* in positions of trust and leadership. As we grow, opportunities to assume leadership positions abound. Some seek them, others shrink from such challenges. At this stage, mentors can be important for would-be leaders. Although experience itself does not always produce learning, experience *plus* careful, honest *reflection* on experience often does. The wise among us extract lessons from experience and especially from our mistakes.

Many corporations have leadership training programs, some send mid-level managers to leadership training seminars. But virtually all large and significant companies take leadership training seriously, as they should.

Such are the stages of leadership; what are the essential skills necessary for the development of good leadership? Efforts to identify core leadership competencies go back many years.[3] The U.S. Office of Personnel Management (OPM) has long wrestled with building a model of leadership skills that remain useful today. In the 1960s, the U.S. Civil Service Commission developed a "General Checklist of Executive Qualifications" (see Table 3.1). This fairly exhaustive list gives us a solid introduction to the overall skills necessary to be an effective leader (the impatient reader may skip over this list of lengthy leadership skills).[4]

Over twenty-five years later (1985), the OPM developed its own list of what skills were necessary to be a good manager (see Table 3.2). In 1992, the OPM came out with a more streamlined list (see Table 3.3). And in 2006, the OPM produced a list of what it considered to be the core executive functions (see Table 3.4).

Effective leaders are confident but not arrogant; know themselves and know the world; communicate clearly and connect with others; exhibit good judgment as well as empathy; recruit and manage a capable team; set priorities and establish goals; have a vision and infuse that vision into a strategy for attainment; are aspirational and empowering; build coalitions and manage organizations; are honest and take others seriously; are change agents and institution builders; are lifelong learners and synthesizers of information; are generalists who learn from specialists; mobilize others and control themselves; have stamina and courage; build and educate; know power and how to use it; travel widely and read extensively; welcome diversity and challenge the status quo; are in touch with their masculine as well as their feminine sides; collaborate and build teams; celebrate success and align their organizations to reward success; learn from their mistakes and recognize their own weaknesses; are hopeful yet tough-minded; are ambitious yet grounded in values; respect followers and respect themselves; build communities yet value alone-time; see the big picture and devise strategies for success; are open-minded and curious; have political savvy and cultural awareness; have energy and determination; are analytical and creative; are decision makers who are deep listeners; are adaptable and context sensitive; are credible and reliable.

TABLE 3.1   General Checklist of Executive Qualifications

Effectiveness with People	General Executive Abilities
1. Ability to represent the organization effectively at all times.	1. Ability to delegate effectively.
2. Ability to gain the confidence of superiors.	2. Effectiveness in checking on results.
3. Ability to handle human relations problems so that morale and productivity are improved.	3. Ability to set priorities effectively.
4. Ability to assign employees to jobs so that optimal utilization of employee abilities results.	4. Ability to use manpower effectively.
5. Willingness to accept subordinates who are not "yes men."	5. Willingness to correct situations when they need improvement and not wait for an emergency.
6. Ability to get the full cooperation of other units.	6. Ability to plan carefully.
7. Ability to deal effectively, even with people who are in opposition. Ability to get people who work for him or her to want to do their best.	7. Ability to handle effectively the administrative details of day-to-day operations.
	8. Effectiveness in presenting budget requests for the unit.
	9. Ability to select highly capable subordinates.
	10. Ability to relate an individual's work to the work of the whole organization.
	11. Ability to take into account the public relations implications of individual actions.
	12. Ability to handle many different problems at the same time.
	13. Ability to work effectively under frustrating conditions.
	14. Ability to properly balance interest in details and in broad problems.
Decision-Making Ability	**Personal Characteristics**
1. Ability to anticipate how people will react to decisions and proposals.	1. Objectivity in considering divergent and new points of view.
2. Ability to absorb new data and concepts quickly.	2. Flexibility in the approach to problems.

(Continued)

TABLE 3.1 (*Continued*)

Decision-Making Ability	Personal Characteristics
3. Recognizes need to first get the facts before making a decision.	3. Reliability—you can depend on what he or she says.
4. Ability to make decisions on the organization of the unit which promotes coordination and efficiency.	4. Willingness to accept responsibility; doesn't pass the buck.
5. Willingness to change the program and methods in order to keep up with current needs and developments.	5. Ability to adjust easily to new situations, problems, and methods.
6. Ability to make decisions on technical problems which keep in mind the latest developments.	6. Ability to keep his or her head in an emergency.
7. Ability to take a broad-gauged approach to problems.	7. Willingness to work to fix things that go wrong instead of making excuses.
8. Ability to spot the key parts of complex problems—not get lost on minor points.	8. Willingness to give an honest report on a problem even if it would hurt him or her personally.
9. Effectiveness in thinking of new approaches to problems.	

TABLE 3.2 OPM Management Excellence Framework*

Management Functions	Management Effectiveness
External Awareness: Keeping up-to-date with key agency policies and priorities, and/or external issues and trends . . . likely to affect the work unit.	*Broad Perspective*: Broad, long-term view; balancing short- and long-term considerations.
Interpretation: Keeping subordinates informed about key . . . policies, priorities, issues, and trends.	*Strategic view*: Collecting/assessing/analyzing information; diagnosis; anticipation; judgment.
Representation: Presenting, explaining, selling, and defending the work unit's activities to the supervisor . . . and persons outside of the agency.	*Environmental Sensitivity*: "Tuned into" agency and its environment; awareness of importance of nontechnical factors.

(*Continued*)

TABLE 3.4 *(Continued)*

- *Strategic Thinking*: Formulates objectives. . . . Capitalizes on opportunities and manages risks.
- *Vision*: Takes a long-term view and builds a shared vision with others; . . . a catalyst for change.

Leading People
- *Conflict management*: Prevents counterproductive confrontations. Resolves conflicts.
- *Leveraging Diversity*: Fosters an inclusive workplace where diversity [is] valued and leveraged.
- *Developing Others*: Develops the ability of others to perform and contribute to the conversation.
- *Team Building*: Fosters team commitment, spirit, pride, and trust. Facilitates cooperation.

Results Driven
- *Accountability*: Holds self and others accountable for high-quality, timely, and cost-effective results.
- *Customer Service*: Meets the needs of internal and external customers; . . . continuous improvement.
- *Decisiveness*: Makes well-informed, effective, and timely decisions.
- *Entrepreneurship*: Identifies new opportunities; . . . developing or improving products or services.
- *Problem Solving*: Analyzes problems; weighs . . . information; . . . evaluates alternative solutions.
- *Technical Credibility*: Appropriately applies . . . specialized expertise.

Business Acumen
- *Financial Management*: Administers the budget, . . . procurement, contracting, . . . cost-benefit thinking.
- *Human Capital Management*: Appropriately recruited, selected, appraised, rewarded [staff].
- *Technology Management*: Makes effective use of technology to achieve results.

Building Coalitions
- *Partnering*: Develops networks, . . . builds alliances.
- *Political Savvy*: Identifies . . . politics that impact the . . . organizational . . . reality and acts accordingly.
- *Influencing/Negotiating*: Persuades others; builds consensus; . . . gains cooperation.

Although all these lists are comprehensive, even exhaustive, the central leadership competencies can be more usefully broken down into twelve key categories:

1. Judgment
2. Emotional Intelligence
3. Empathy
4. Flexibility and Balance
5. Moral Courage and Compass
6. Self and World Knowledge
7. Communication Skills
8. Recognize and Develop Talent
9. Articulate a Compelling Vision
10. Adapt
11. Learn from Mistakes
12. Contextual Intelligence

These twelve essential skills, if properly developed, may lead to what Aristotle referred to as *phronesis*, the ultimate goal of all leaders, and a subject we return to later.

☐ Judgment

There is no more important leadership skill than sound judgment.

We are all children of the Enlightenment, the Age of Reason, a time when we believed that humans were capable of self-governing because they were capable of rational thought. The government of the United States is grounded in this belief, as Alexander Hamilton so aptly noted in the very first of *The Federalist Papers*:

> It has been frequently remarked that it seems to have been reserved to the people of this country, by their conduct and example, to decide the important question, whether societies of men are really capable or not of establishing good government from reflection and choice, or whether they are forever destined to depend for their political constitutions on accident and force.[5]

"Reflection and thought," the very basis of rationality. But do we flatter ourselves when we posit such a praiseworthy self-portrait? Are humans *really* rational beings?

The entire basis of the science of politics in which I was trained (as were economists, sociologists, and many others) is the belief or assumption that we are rational beings who can make rational decisions. If so, our actions are somewhat predictable, and if predictable, one can make forecasts or predictions of how humans will behave. But is this image so?

In the past few decades, challenges to the rational actor model have emerged that call into question the very basis of these sciences. The primary challenge has come from the field of what many call *brain science*, a branch of neurology (the study of the nervous system).

Just what do we mean by judgment? As Nan Keohane, former President of Duke University, writes, "we can understand judgment as a distinctive mental faculty or skill, a way of approaching deliberation and decision making that combines experience, intuition, taste, and intelligence."[6]

The new thinking on judgment and decision-making suggests that there are three key sources of input that contribute to a decision: the *head* (the rational part of our brains); the *heart* (the emotional side of our brains); and the *gut* (the intuitive part of our brains; see Table 3.5). These three parts, rather than being in conflict can—in sound decision-making—work together in positive, cooperative, and constructive ways.

Good decision-making requires *both* the rational brain *and* the emotional brain to work together. As Jonah Lehrer puts it:

> What we discover when we look at the brain is that the horses and the charioteer depend upon each other. If it weren't for our emotions, reason wouldn't exist at all and the process of thinking requires feelings, for feelings are what let us understand all the information that we can't directly comprehend. Reason without emotion is impotent.[7]

TABLE 3.5   Decision Making: We Make Decisions Based on Three Factors

	The Head	**The Heart**	**The Gut**
Type:	Rational	Emotional	Intuitive
Source:	The Enlightenment	Neuroscience	Educated Guesses Built on Experience
Derived From:	Age of Reason, Rationality	Feelings and Emotions	Experience Reflected Upon and Internalized
Basis:	Logic Based	Passion Based	Experience Based
Fields:	Philosophy/Math	Art/Poetry	Self-Awareness

In thinking, the keys are openness, self-awareness, balance, flexibility, and metacognition.

Still, there are a number of decision-making traps into which we often fall. Our brains are energy drains—they need tons of energy to function at a high level. So to save energy, the brain takes shortcuts that make us prone to self-delusion. *Framing* is a particularly vexing problem for decision makers. Our choices are susceptible to the way options are presented to us. Once we accept a frame, we funnel our ideas and options through that frame, excluding other options. For example, *never* look at the sticker price when buying a car. If you do, that dollar amount will frame the negotiations, and you will begin the process already having given up valuable territory. If the salesman can get you to start from the sticker price, he has you. Better to go online and find the dealer cost (much lower) and insist on starting there—it is a better frame (for you at least).

Hubris is another dangerous cognitive trap. It means pride or arrogance and an overestimation of one's own power or competence. One could see the hubris involved in the George W. Bush administration's lead-up to the war in Iraq in 2003 when they insisted that "we would be greeted as liberators," and "the oil money from Iraq's wells would pay for the war," and it will be a slam dunk, and "we know where the WMD (weapons of mass destruction) are." Such blind overconfidence led the administration away from doing its due diligence, and by the time we realized how wrong we were, thousands of lives and millions of dollars had been spent.[8]

Groupthink is yet another common decision making problem. When part of a group, we often value harmony, collegiality, belonging, and group membership over hard analysis. We are hesitant to go against the group for fear we will be excluded, or divided. So we go along, keep our doubts to ourselves, and "fit in." At times the group can even go so far as to make it clear that dissent is seen as disloyalty. This narrows options and can lead to tragic mistakes.[9]

Leaders make decisions with limited and often confusing information in an atmosphere of deep uncertainty. This *bounded rationality* should cause us to be humble about our ability to make good decisions. Any decision involves risk and is at best an educated guess. And there are recurring patterns of incompetence even the best of us are prone to make. Thus, all leaders need a large dose of humility. We are not as smart, or as rational as we believe. Good judgment is important, and so too might be reflection and learning from experience, reliable and diverse information, an open and alert mind, critical thinking skills, creativity, and a strategic sensibility.

In the end, leaders confront three types of decision challenges: *individual* (decision traps, hubris, ideology, information absorption, emotion, etc.); *group* (where our team degenerates into groupthink, yes-men and sycophants, group insulation, partiality, etc.); and *organizational* (bureaucratic inertia or competition, poor information flow, unclear communication, etc.).[10]

In general, leaders will need stamina, intelligence, optimism, creativity, honesty, and a bit of cunning; wisdom; courage; a sense of humor; empathy; a healthy sense of self-esteem; compassion; caring; a thick skin and a rugged stamina; a power sense; a knowledge of self, the world, and the organization; a sense of history; the ability to communicate and persuade; political and managerial skills; the ability to judge others and appropriately delegate responsibility; vision; quick thinking; self-confidence but not arrogance; the ability to put team members together and make them work in concert; and emotional intelligence. A long list indeed.

Leadership is the game of the grandmaster of chess. You must see the entire board; calculate many restraints, challenges, and opportunities along the way; calibrate and then recalibrate; and design and redesign your strategic approach as the game evolves. The hand you draw may be a good one or a bad one; you may be able with skill to improve your hand; you may be able to bluff your way to victory.

Winning involves a combination of luck and skill. Napoleon used to say, "Find me a lucky general!" And the great golfer Gary Player used to say, "The more I practice, the luckier I get." Of course, both knew that one can help force fortune's hand with hard work and skill, that great leaders *make* their luck as much as fortune smiles upon them. The basketball player who seems to pick up cheap baskets is called lucky, but her movement away from the ball creates opportunities for her to take advantage of loose balls and broken defenses. It is skill that creates opportunities for fortune to smile upon her. She is in the right place at the right time, not by accident but by design. As Ralph Waldo Emerson wrote, "Shallow men believe in luck. Strong men believe in cause and effect." And Gracian reminded us of *the art of being lucky*.

> There are rules of luck and the wise do not leave it all to chance. Luck can be assisted by care. Some content themselves with placing themselves confidently at the gate of fortune, waiting till she opens it. Others do better, and press forward and profit by their clever boldness, reaching the goddess and winning her favor in the wings of their virtue and valor. But a true philosophy has no other umpire than virtue and insight—for there is no good or bad luck except wisdom and foolishness.[11]

Being attuned to opportunities is a prerequisite for success. In this, it is often wise—in chess as in leadership—to make the first move. Plutarch, in *The Rise and Fall of Athens,* noted this exchange between Eurybiades and Themistocles: " 'You know, Themistocles, at the games they thrash anybody who starts before the signal,' to which Themistocles replied, 'Yes, but they do not crown anybody who gets left at the post.' "[12] But in this, as in all things, *think.* As Gracian warned, "Think beforehand. Today, for tomorrow, and even for many days hence. The greatest foresight consists in determining beforehand the time of trouble. For the provident there are no mischances and for the careful no narrow escapes."[13]

For successful leadership, skill is important, but skill is never enough. Even the most skilled individuals face formidable roadblocks. Skill helps determine the extent to which a leader takes advantage of or is bound by circumstances, but circumstances or the environment set the parameters of what is possible regarding leadership. President Reagan referred to the "window of opportunity," his way of talking about how open or closed circumstances were for exercising presidential leadership. If one is dealt a weak hand, there is only so much that skill can do. But if one is dealt four aces, what Machiavelli called *fortuna* (fortune), not skill, determines the outcome. This is not to say that skill is unimportant. But in the constellation of factors that contribute to success or failure, skill is but one determinant.

Machiavelli spent a great deal of attention on fortune. Good luck is a valuable asset, but one can never rely on it. We are all familiar with the story of the princess, who, coming upon a frog, kissed it, and transformed it into a prince. Less familiar, but more common, is the less frequently told story of the princess who kissed a toad, and it remained a toad. If you are kissed by good fortune, so much the better. But it is best to make your own luck and not passively rely on fortune.

But more than luck is involved here. Skill (what Machiavelli was referring to when he wrote of *virtu*) matters as well. And what skills must the effective leader possess? Machiavelli answered the question with an analogy. The skilled leader must play both the lion *and* the fox. The lion was strong, a great fighter who instilled fear in rivals. But the lion lacked cunning, wisdom, and the ability to fool an adversary. The fox is the skilled manipulator, who by cunning, guile, and deception was able to misdirect an adversary. Although the fox was not a master in battle, it was skilled in the art of deception and wise in the choice of tactics.

The great leader combines the skills of the lion and the fox. As Machiavelli stated in *The Prince,* "as a prince is forced to know how to act like a beast, he must learn from the fox and the lion. Those who simply act like lions are stupid."

☐ Emotional Intelligence

Wechsler writes that "intelligence is the aggregate or global capacity of the individual to act purposefully, to think rationally, and to deal effectively with his environment."[14] Social intelligence, according to E. L. Thorndike is "the ability to understand men and women, boys and girls—to act wisely in human relations."[15] When one adds emotion to the mix, we get closer to what is meant by emotional intelligence, and its impact on adaptive and maladaptive behaviors.

Salovey and Mayer argue that emotional intelligence is a "subset of social intelligence that involves the *ability to monitor one's own and others' feelings and emotions, to discriminate among them and to use this information to guide one's thinking and actions* (italics in original)." It is a form of contextual and interpersonal intelligence that involves diagnosis (appraisal of situation, people, and self), self-regulation, appropriate emotional response, and feedback evaluation. And as Salovey and Mayer note, "When people approach life tasks with emotional intelligence, they should be at an advantage for solving problems adaptively."[16]

Generally, emotional intelligence is the ability (which can be learned) to accurately perceive, understand, and empathize with the feelings and needs of others; to confine our emotions and responses to appropriate behaviors given the situation; to express ourselves clearly and sympathetically; and to maximize our responses to people and circumstances. It is about self-mastery, about knowing yourself, controlling your emotions, channeling those emotions in constructive ways, and recognizing others and contexts. Emotional intelligence is about using to the fullest both the intrapersonal and the interpersonal. In short, it is about using our emotions intelligently. It begins with self-awareness and extends to other awareness, then to context awareness, and finally to a healthy and constructive response or action.[17]

A person adept in emotional intelligence is able to accurately perceive others, capably express him- or herself, comprehensively understand the context or situation, control and manage their emotions, communicate clearly, and apply a reasonable solution to the problem. A leader skilled in emotional intelligence can control him- or herself and influence others. Aristotle, in a pre-emotional intelligence age, well understood the emotional intelligence dilemma that successful leaders, and successful people, must come to grips with. He wrote,

> Anyone can become angry—that is easy. But to be angry with the right person, to the right degree, at the right time, for the right purpose, and in the right way—this is not easy.[18]

Not easy, yet essential for self-control and sound leadership decision making. It is emotional intelligence or emotional competence (empathy, social skills, self-control, and self-confidence, adaptability, self-awareness, self-regulation) that make one successful.

Daniel Goleman notes:

> The most effective leaders are alike in one crucial way: They all have a huge degree of what has come to be known as emotional intelligence. It's not that IQ and technical skills are irrelevant. They do matter, but mainly as "threshold capabilities" that is, they are the entry-level requirements for executive positions. But my research, along with other recent studies, clearly shows that emotional intelligence is the sine qua non of leadership. Without it, a person can have the best training in the world, an incisive, analytical mind, and an endless supply of smart ideas, but he still won't make a great leader.[19]

Goleman insists that emotional intelligence can be learned as well as internalized—with practice. Or, as Aristotle reminds us, "Excellence is an art won by training and habituation. We do not act rightfully because we have virtue or excellence, but we rather have these because we have acted rightly. We are what we repeatedly do. Excellence, then, is not an act but a habit."[20]

Three sets of skills are useful in leadership: technical skill (mastering your field along with planning and management skills); cognitive skill (reasoning, analytical ability, sound judgment); and emotional intelligence (self-management, empathy, the ability to work with others). All three are useful, yet one skill stands out above the rest.

Again, one can learn to become a more effective leader. One does this in the same way one becomes a better person, or a better baseball player, or a better pianist: deliberative practice. An effective leader (like a great baseball player) develops habits of excellence. The old adage, "You are what you eat" can be applied to leaders (and ballplayers): You are what you do. If you engage in repeated, focused, disciplined practices or arts aimed at excellence, over time you get better, grow, and develop habits of excellence. . . . It becomes part of you.

Derek Jeter is the greatest shortstop of his age because (1) he was naturally gifted (but then, loads of people are born with these gifts and do little with them); (2) he was highly motivated; (3) he was focused and disciplined; (4) he worked extremely hard; (5) he was well coached and temperamentally prepared to learn from good coaches; (6) he then repeatedly engaged in deliberate practice; (7) received feedback (from coaches); (8) was dogged in his pursuit of excellence; and (9) developed habits of excellence that over time, became a part of the fabric of his being.

When I was young, I played baseball—a lot. And, in all immodesty, I was darn good at it. So good, in fact, that at age 16, a Pittsburgh Pirates scout got me on a semi-pro baseball team—Jess Cox All-Stars—in Pasadena, California. On that team were several minor league players, among them was Darrel Evans who ended up hitting 414 major league home runs as a Giant, Brave, and Tiger.

I had aspirations to play centerfield for the New York Yankees, but ended up at first base—my "natural" position. Broken ankles in two consecutive seasons put an end to my dream (as did the curveball), and I ended up a professor not a player. Ah, what a loss for baseball.

Why tell this story? Because when I was growing up, you learned baseball by playing baseball. There were coaches of course, but they were usually one of the kids' dads who had an afternoon here or there to devote to serving his community. This meant that I was given very little instruction in the fundamentals of baseball: how to position my feet around first base, how to hook slide, how to round a base, etc. I say this not to demean the fine men who coached but to set the situation.

Around the time I was in high school in the late 1960s—switching now to basketball—some of my teammates were talking about going to John Wooden's summer basketball camp to improve their skills. And several of the students from wealthier families did (yes, I'm just a little bitter) and markedly improved their performance. It was then that something clicked. If I wanted to be better at X, it meant *expert coaching*. Yes, baseball and basketball were fun, and I had a God-given talent, but to really rise I needed:

Natural ability,
Motivation,
Hard work,
Expert instruction, and
Deliberate, focused practice.

At a certain point, it wasn't about who was the more gifted athlete, or who worked hardest, it was about who refined their skills to the highest level. Some athletes were more skilled and better trained, and developed higher technique levels. Being well-coached made a difference. I could not make up, in hard work, or even natural ability, the training gap that developed the technique of the other athletes.

TABLE 3.6 The Six Qs of Leadership

Abbreviation	Title	Level of Importance
IQ	Intelligence Quotient	15%
EQ	Emotional Quotient	40%
CQ	Character Quotient	10%
XQ	Executive Function/ Quotient	15%
LQ	Liberal Arts Quotient	10%
EQ	Experience Quotient	10%

The lesson here, of course, is that we all need expert coaching. Hard work matters. So does natural talent. But proper coaching is the leg up we need to excel. If Derek Jeter needs a coach why don't you? If Michael Jordan needed coaching, why are you any different?[21]

Perhaps surprisingly, there is *no* correlation between IQ and leadership. As long as they have an average or higher IQ, they are leadership material. More important than IQ is emotional intelligence. Emotional control, situational awareness, self-knowledge, and other awareness have much more to do with leadership than IQ (see Table 3.6).

Emotional intelligence involves:

- Self-Awareness—Awareness of one's emotions
- Other Awareness—Sensitivity of the emotions of others
- Self-Management—The ability to self-regulate
- Social Awareness—Understanding of groups and context
- Relationship Management—The ability to form healthy, positive relations with others
- Empathy—Feeling with and for others

These factors are integrated into the "6 Qs" universe of leadership development to form a matrix of desirable—and developable—skills.

Executive Function: By *executive function*, we mean a cognitive process whereby we develop skills at decision making, problem solving, mental flexibility, self-management, reasoning, and working memory. The development of executive function begins early in childhood as babies, and later children learn how to read situations and develop healthy models of decision making and problem solving.

Intelligence Quotient: This is a numerical score derived from standardized tests. It measures general intelligence, and these tests are seen as a predictor of educational achievement. However, IQ alone is a poor prediction of happiness, success, or accomplishment. IQ is important as setting a baseline which, once reached, opens doors for other factors to intervene (e.g., emotional intelligence) and be applied to decision making and judgment.

Character Quotient: As leadership involves trust, all leaders are put under a character microscope. There is considerable disagreement about how character impacts leadership. Some believe that a leader's personal behavior is and should be a part of our assessment of their public performance. Others believe that what is important in a leader is how they perform in office, not what they do in private. Clearly, some of our most important and successful leaders led questionable private lives. Perhaps by public character, we should discern the extent to which leaders fight for what is right, speak truth to power, and stand up for fairness and justice.

Experience Quotient: Although not absolutely necessary for success, in general, having substantial experience increases one's ability to perform complex tasks. Experience is one thing, but what is most important is what one learns from that experience. Merely being there is not enough.

Liberal Arts Education Quotient: Most successful leaders are generalists who are capable of communicating clearly, thinking critically, managing self and others, and understanding what is right. There is no better preparation for leadership than a demanding liberal arts education.

The search for the ideal leader goes on, with scholars desperately trying to isolate the leadership gene that produces magical results. The problem is, effective leaders come in all shapes and sizes; some are introverts, others extroverts, some ooze charisma whereas others seem shy and analytical. Attempts to identify, through *trait theory*, those traits and practices that lead to breakthrough leadership have proved unsatisfying. So what makes a great leader great?

☐ Empathy

If good judgment is the most important quality a leader can have, empathy is the most important quality a human being can have. It is empathy that opens all the doors to a well-adjusted, happy life, a life truly worth living.

Empathy is our ability to identify other people's feelings and to be *other-oriented* in the sense that one is able to "get into another person's shoes" and—to a large extent—see the world through their eyes. I often tell my graduating students that many of them are on the verge of making the most important decision of their lives: to whom they will wed. And I tell my students that the first and most important things to look for in a would-be spouse is empathy. If they do not have empathy, run like the wind.

In a leader, empathy allows one to connect with followers, and to see and feel their needs, fears, hopes, and concerns. Good leaders accurately read situations (context) and accurately read and care deeply about people (empathy). If leadership is about people, followers, and building trust, the development of empathy skills can make one a far better leader.[22]

☐ Flexibility and Balance

As Charles Darwin reminded us, it is not the strongest of the species that survive, but the one most adaptable and responsive to change. To adapt, one needs to be flexible and balanced. Niccolo Machiavelli enjoined his prince to be flexible enough to accurately read the situation, then be the lion or the fox depending on what the context required.

Rigidity is the enemy of leadership; flexibility its ally. George W. Bush liked to tell audiences that he stuck to his guns, didn't respond to poll numbers, did what he thought was right, didn't change his mind, and didn't bend with the wind. This is a short step from rigidity, inflexibility, and close-mindedness. Mature individuals are capable of change, of adapting, of adjusting, of balancing competing interests, and of being flexible. Life is about change. We change because circumstances change. We must be open to change when new information reaches us, when the assumptions on which we based our actions prove in the end to have been wrong, and when things do not work out as we hoped or planned. Sticking to a mistake is the sign of inflexibility and closed mindedness. Thus we must be *high-flex* in a *high-flux* world.

Great leaders have the ability to *style-flex*. That is, they can adjust their dance to fit the music being played. They are sensitive to and in tune with the needs and demands of the times and situation. They recognize when to push and when to back away, when to lead and when to follow, when to speak and when to remain quiet, when to force the action and when to refrain. As the Roman politician Cicero said, in politics the means can vary from time to time while the end remains the same; "I believe in moving with the times," and that

> [u]nchanging consistency of standpoint has never been con-
> sidered a virtue in great statesmen. At sea it is good sailing to
> run before the gale, even if the ship cannot make harbor; but
> if she can make harbor by changing tack, only a fool would
> risk shipwreck by holding to the original course rather than
> change it and still reach his destination.[23]

As Sun Tzu reminded us in *The Art of War*, "[V]ictory in war is not repetitious, but adapts its form endlessly. . . . So a military force has no constant formation, water has no constant shape: the ability to gain victory by changing and adapting according to the opponent is called genius."[24]

Perhaps no American politician better practiced this art than Franklin D. Roosevelt, who once said,

> You know I am a juggler, and I never let my right hand know
> what my left hand does. . . . I may have one policy for Europe
> and one diametrically opposite for North and South America,
> I may be entirely inconsistent, and furthermore I am perfectly
> willing to mislead and tell untruths if it will help win the war.[25]

Few people talk about how physically and emotionally taxing leadership is. It demands a lot. Few have the physical stamina and the emotional strength to be in top form over extended periods of time.

Leadership is high stress. It is physically exhausting. It requires physical stamina and emotional flexibility. Few leaders come by these naturally. It must be cultivated, developed, learned. One way to both understand what is required of leaders and also for leaders to develop the attributes needed for effective leadership, is through yoga.

The word yoga means "union" in Sanskrit (the ancient language of India, where yoga originated). It is meant to signify the union of *mind, body,* and *spirit*. It brings them into harmony. In modern terms, yoga is a series of stretches—gentle and challenging—designed to promote flexibility, reduce stress, develop stamina, improve balance, encourage unity, and strengthen focus. And isn't that what we want of leaders as well as healthy individuals?

For centuries, yoga has helped people clear their minds, giving them a sense of equanimity. "Although yoga is physical in nature, its benefits are both physical and emotional. On the emotional side, yoga is a tremendous stress reducer," writes Richard Carlson, "It balances the body-mind-spirit connections, giving you a feeling of ease and peace."[26]

Effective leaders and effective individuals are flexible, not rigid; they can deal effectively with and control stress; they are physically capable; they promote balance and are able to unify the different elements of mind, body, and their humanity; and they bring about clearer focus.[27]

There are "eight limbs" of yoga. Each limb builds upon the limb that precedes it. First, *Yama*, the five ethical guidelines that govern our dealings with others. They include *Ahimsa* (do not steal), *Brahmacharya* (do not lust after others), and *Aparigraha* (noncovetness).

The second limb of yoga is *Niyama*, the five ethical guidelines toward the self. These include *Saucha* (cleanliness), *Suntosa* (contentment), *Tapas* (sustained practice), *Svadhyaya* (self study), and *Isvara prandihana* (surrender to god).

The third limb is *Asana* or the practice of yoga postures and poses. This leads—both figuratively and literally to stretching and developing flexibility. Here we see the contrast between the practice of yoga poses and weight-training. Yoga practice leads to flexibility and balance; weight-training leads to buildup of muscle bulk and rigidity. For the leader—and most individuals—the health (physical and emotional) benefits of yoga far outweigh the benefits of weight lifting.

The fourth limb is *Pranayama*. This involves the practice of breathing exercises designed to consciously focus attention on self and bringing focus to breath. Fifth is *Pratyahara*, or the withdrawal of the senses from the distractions of the world, allowing one to focus within. Sixth is *Dharana* or concentration, the ability to deeply focus uninterrupted by outside distractions. Seven is *Dhyana* or meditation. Finally, there is *Samadhi* or happiness. In yoga it is the merging of self to the universe. How then does yoga meld with leadership? Yoga gives the leader tools and some of the skills necessary for effective leadership. It prepares one for the stresses and challenges that will confront a leader. Yoga puts the leader in a better position to control oneself and constructively manage the tasks of leadership.

☐ Moral Courage and Compass

Leaders help manage the values of a group or organization. They set—by words and deeds—the limits on acceptable behavior, signal the ethical level of the group, and model behavior for the organization. Leaders set a tone, give followers clues regarding the type of behavior that is acceptable, even rewarded in the organization.

The most important signal to a follower as to what behaviors are permitted, encouraged, or discouraged come from the leader. If a leader stresses the importance of honorable behavior, followers will follow that lead. If the boss cuts moral corners and displays a win-at-all costs mentality, followers will cut corners. Leadership matters.

Richard Nixon made it clear to his subordinates that the political environment was filled with people out to destroy the administration and that they were going to employ a win-at-all-costs strategy. This opened the door for some very unsavory behavior (burglaries, break-ins, extortion, etc.).[28] Nixon created an atmosphere in which his subordinates believed they were doing the president's bidding, and in a way, Nixon's message—that moral corner-cutting was permissible—seeped down to those working on his behalf. It was a recipe for moral failure.[29]

Leaders must know what to fight for. This requires a moral compass sensitive to the demands of fairness, the pain of the forgotten, and the values of the community. But knowing what to fight for is not enough, the effective leader must also have the political sensitivity and acumen to know when to join the fight, and the courage to confront injustice.

☐ Self-Knowledge/World Knowledge

As mentioned, the ancient Greeks enjoined us to "know thyself." Only by leading an *examined life* could we hope to know justice and act justly.

In his excellent book *On Becoming a Leader*, Warren Bennis emphasizes the importance of both self and world knowledge in the development of effective leaders.[30] The former is essential for personal growth and development. The latter enables one to effectively navigate the complexities of the divisive world around us.

World knowledge is essential for leadership in today's interdependent, connected world. Being able to read diverse situations, know how others think, what they believe, what their hopes and fears are, all bring us closer to the knowledge—and empathy—necessary for making sound judgments.

The study of history, other cultures, and religions, other traditions and practices not only makes us more complete, it better equips us for dealing with diversity. And tomorrow's world will be more complex, more diverse, and even more challenging than our age.

The United States can sometimes be accused of hegemonic arrogance in assuming that as the world's only superpower, we are allowed to dictate to the world, believing there is precious little the rest of the world can teach us. Such arrogance can quite literally be deadly, as the tragic war in Vietnam confirms. If we are to govern the world, we must know the world. Other cultures and nations have much to offer, if only we would seek to learn.[31]

☐ Communication: Inter-/Intrapersonal Skills

Effective leaders are good communicators, They speak clearly, write clearly, and think clearly. They listen deeply. Many are good at self-promotion and self-dramatization. Many have a singular message to deliver.

Ronald Reagan, for all his faults as a manager, was an effective leader because he had a distinct vision, expressed it with sincerity, clarity, and strength, and was able to connect with his audience. Reagan is a good example of nature and nurture working in unison. He possessed a natural charm, soothing voice, was tall and handsome (a former movie actor), *and* he worked hard (trained and experienced in front of the camera) to develop his interpersonal skills.

Leadership is in large part about persuasion, and the ability to communicate clearly, sincerely, with strength of conviction and passion, helps leaders induce a following. It is sometimes a branch of show business.

Among the most prized communication skills is active *listening*. Part of empathy and emotional intelligence, deep listening gives you a sense of your audience—be it one person or a large group. Being able to "read a crowd" allows the leader to tailor his or her style or content to the context.

☐ Recognize, Train, and Reward Talent

Leaders can't do it alone. They need a cadre of talented, committed colleagues and followers to accomplish their goals.

An effective leader knows, as has been said before, who should be on the bus, who should be off the bus, who should be in what seat on the bus, and in what direction the bus ought to be headed. And they know how to put all this together into an integrated whole.

Team-building, talent-recognizing, and talent-rewarding are key skills for the effective leader. The effective organization attracts talented people (one of the reasons Google is so effective is that the most talented people *want* to work there), trains them, praises them, gives them freedom and responsibility, and amply rewards them for their contributions.

And at the opposite end of the scale, effective organizations—just as importantly weed out the bad seeds.[32] Troublemakers breed like rabbits and can take down an organization if you let them. Throw them off the bus, or you will soon find yourself under the bus.

☐ Articulate a Compelling Vision

The Great American philosopher who held court at stadiums across the nation, Yogi Berra once said, "If you don't know where you're going, you might end up somewhere else." All organizations need a sense of direction, a goal. In the corporate world, the primary goal is profit. In the political world, the goal is contested territory, with competing claims for the *where*, *to*, and *how* of the state.

One of the first tasks of a leader is to define the prism through which the people see and understand reality. The public often needs complex issues reduced to simpler and more manageable terms it can better understand. The people need to see where they are going. The leader's job is to illuminate the path, chart the course, and enlighten the constituents on where you wish to lead them. The path you light can be either dim or bright. If you articulate and sell a compelling vision, you can become a transforming leader.

Cardinal Richelieu once said, "Experience shows that, if one foresees from far away the designs to be undertaken, one can act with speed when the moment comes to execute them."[33] A vision allows us to see where we wish to go, and when the moment is right, to move in that direction. Vision is purpose exposed and made whole. The Book of Proverbs (28:18) reminds us, "where there is no vision, the people perish."

A vision is a dream of the future, a dream that is realistic enough to appear attainable, different enough to inspire, and attractive enough to gain commitment. It is about selling hope: This is what tomorrow can be, this is what it looks like, this is how we can get there, this is what it will cost, and this is our ultimate reward. A vision grabs your attention, stirs the imagination, and appeals to what is the best in us.

Visionary leaders continue to have an effect long after they are gone. For example, it has been over fifty years since John F. Kennedy was killed and over forty since the death of Martin Luther King Jr., yet the memories of their leadership—the power of their ideas, the force of their rhetoric, and impact of their words—remain influential forces even today.

Victor Hugo reminds us that, "There is nothing so powerful as an idea whose time has come." One of the primary tasks of a leader is to discern the dominant needs of the times then develop and articulate a vision to meet those needs.

Leaders such as Vaclev Havel of Czechoslovakia, Nelson Mandela of South Africa, Abraham Lincoln of the United States, Bill Gates of Microsoft, and Jesus Christ of Nazareth, demonstrated the power of a compelling vision when matched with skill, savvy, persistence, and a dose of luck.

Such leaders often relate to followers through stories (Lincoln, for example) or parables (Jesus). They paint word pictures, articulate what is often hidden or unspoken deep within the people, they build hope. As Father Theodore Hesburgh, former President of Notre Dame University noted, "The very essence of leadership is (that) you have to have a vision. It's got to be a vision you articulate clearly and forcefully on every occasion. You can't blow an uncertain trumpet."[34]

A vision is aspirational. It guides action; is about the future; draws people to its logic and premise; is about excellence and empowerment; animates behavior; is goal oriented; defines meaning and shapes the future; gives the leader and citizens a shared sense of purpose; empowers leaders and citizens alike; develops mutual respect between the leader and the led; simplifies complex reality; provides meaning and purpose; articulates what is often hidden and the hopes and dreams of a people; reveals the essence of a people; translates hope into action; is practical; inspires hope; is about erecting a new and better tomorrow; challenges the people to do more, be more, and be better; is a picture of the mind's eye of what can be; gives direction to society; and is about the big picture. A vision tells us who we are, where we are, which way to go, and what we hope to create. Visions can change reality.

As T. E. Lawrence (of Arabia) noted,

> All men dream; but not equally.
> Those who dream by night in the dusty recesses of their minds
> Awake to find that it was vanity;
> But the dreamers of day are dangerous men,
> That they may act their dreams with open eyes to make it
>   possible.[35]

☐ Adaption

Ron Heifetz rightly draws our attention to the adapting role many leaders play.[36] Where problems have a technical solution, leadership is hardly necessary. We simply apply the right solution to our problem. If a heart artery is blocked, a trained doctor can open that artery and fix the problem.

And yet, the doctor has not truly solved the problem, only temporarily fixed the artery. The real problem is that the patient smokes two packs of cigarettes a day, is obese and eats a diet rich in fats, does not exercise, and leads a high-stress life.

So how do we help the patient? He needs to change. He needs to stop smoking, lose weight, eat a healthy diet, exercise, and do yoga to reduce stress.

Leadership comes into play when we do not have a technical solution to our problem and need a new strategy to help us adapt. Adaptive challenges are recurrent problems outside our current repertoire; we are unable to devise a technical quick-fix; we need to adapt our behavior to deal with this challenge or threat.

Leaders help us recognize where the old or technical solutions fall short, identify needed behavioral alterations to the status quo, mobilize the public to change, empower and assist this transition, and develop and promote a vision of an alternative future.

The current environmental crisis is a good example of leaders misdiagnosing the problem by treating an adaptive challenge as a technical problem. "Oh," we are told, "if we only would use less gas." Although getting better gas mileage from our cars, driving less, etc. are all good, these technical quick-fixes are insufficient to meet the real challenge we face. To truly tackle the environmental crisis *we* need to change; *we* need to alter our lifestyle.

In the 1970s, when President Jimmy Carter attempted to get the American public to face the energy/environmental crisis, he was met with a chorus of criticism. We didn't want to change; we were unwilling to settle for less. We demanded a technical solution to our problem. Lamentably, in the past forty years, we have yet to find that technical solution.

Now, we face potential catastrophe. Where is the adaptive leadership coming from on this issue? Not from our leaders or office-holders. The real adaptive leadership is percolating up from citizen groups and activists. Such adaptive leadership by office-holders seems too risky, too costly, too dangerous. They cower in the face of our demands for a comfortable lifestyle. They pander to our appetites and have forfeited leadership for fear of being too far ahead of the curve. And yet, truly adaptive leadership from the top as well as support from the citizens, will be absolutely necessary if we are to confront, reverse, and solve this crisis.

Adaptive leadership can be risky, yet it can be necessary and rewarding. Getting us to face up to the crisis ahead and offering adaptive changes to help us meet these challenges is what leading is all about. We must empower adaptive leadership, giving our elected officials permission to give us the bad news along with adaptive solutions. Adaptive leadership will not emerge until and unless we allow it to.

☐ Setbacks and Mistakes

Thomas Edison made nearly 3,000 mistakes before he hit on the right formula for the light bulb. Inventors and creators failed far more than they succeeded, and the mark of real success is persistence and drive. If the great inventors had given up after a few failures, we might still be in the dark ages.[37]

No one likes to fail, but we all fail, often. The key is: What do we *learn* from failure? Do we profit by it, or do we become paralyzed by it? Does it spark a new line of thought or relegate us to self-defeat? Does it make us shrink from future battles or inspire us to seek and alternate route? Does it push us to grow or to sit back and accept less? Abraham Lincoln lost more elections than he won; Winston Churchill failed far more times than he succeeded.

"Try again, fail again, fail better," Samuel Beckett enjoined us. In truly successful people, failure is often the gateway to greatness.

Those who profit most from failure share certain characteristics: They develop a kind of *learned optimism,* not a blind optimism but an informed optimism grounded in reality. They apply conscientious analytical skills to understanding the causes of failure; that is, they think about and reflect on why they failed. They are capable of being open minded and learning from their mistakes, rather than denying them, making excuses, running away from, or blaming others for their failures. They bring others into the process and do not face problems alone; that is, they seek out mentors, guides, teachers, and coaches to help them through their problems. And perhaps surprisingly, those most capable of learning from failures are people raised under more stressful family conditions and not in "happy homes." In those more stressful families, children were often given greater responsibility at an earlier age than one might have expected. Happy upbringings, it seems, lead us to have a type of Pollyanna view and do not prepare us for the hellish tests life will throw at us.

When Richard Nixon was first confronted with the Watergate dilemma, he made it into a scandal and then a constitutional crisis by covering up his mistakes with crimes; when Ronald Reagan was caught in the Iran-Contra scandal, at first he denied it, then he tried to manage the scandal; when Bill Clinton was caught in the Monica

Lewinsky sex scandal, he lied about it. And during the presidency of George W. Bush, the leak of the name of a CIA operative led to a scandal that was compounded when top administration officials lied about it, leading to criminal charges, and yet another presidential embarrassment. In all these cases, the cover up was worse than the crime. None of these presidents learned the lessons of the past. Remember the old Latin warning: "abyssus abyssum invocat," one misstep leads to another.

A good president has people around him who can tell him when he is traveling down the wrong path. It isn't easy to tell this to the president, or corporate leader, but you must have a few trusted advisors who can be blunt with you. Former President Gerald Ford (1979) has as good a take on this than anyone:

> Few people, with the possible exception of his wife, will ever tell a president that he is a fool. There's a majesty to the office that inhibits even your closest friends from saying what is really on their minds. They won't tell you that you just made a lousy speech or bungled a chance to get your point across . . . yet the President—any President—needs to hear straight talk. He needs to be needled once in a while, if only to be brought down from the false pedestal that the office provides. He needs to be told that he is, after all, only another human being with the same virtues and weaknesses as anyone else. And he needs to be reminded of this constantly if he's going to keep his perspective . . .[38]

If you make a mistake, admit it, and admit it fully and immediately. Take full responsibility right away. When George W. Bush blundered in the federal response to Hurricane Katrina, his first reaction was to blame everyone but himself. Then he issued the generic "mistakes were made" statement. A week later, when he finally took responsibility for his failures, it was too little too late. His adversaries were handed a golden opportunity to make him look insensitive and out of touch. The Bush administration was put in an unwinnable position as they tried to undo the damage done by the president. But as they scrambled, they only further dug a hole for the beleaguered president. Do as John F. Kennedy did after the Bay of Pigs fiasco: take full and immediate responsibility, try to learn from your mistakes, and move on. If you take responsibility, most people will understand, appreciate your honesty, maybe even forgive you. If you cover up, you will be—and you will deserve to be—crushed.

The great Samurai Hagakure wrote the following:

It is said that one should not hesitate to correct himself when he has made a mistake. If he corrects himself without the least bit of delay, his mistakes will quickly disappear. But when he tries to cover up a mistake, it will become all the more unbecoming and painful.[39]

The goal, of course, is to do the right thing, and to execute it effectively. But mistakes happen. And even the best and the brightest make mistakes. Effective leaders take responsibility for their mistakes, own up to them, try to right them. Ineffective leaders blame others or have so little self-awareness that they are incapable of seeing, not to mention admitting mistakes.

At an April 13, 2004, news conference, President George W. Bush was asked to name the biggest mistake he made after 9/11, and what lesson he had learned. Responding, Bush joked, "I wish you'd have given me this written question ahead of time so I could plan for it." After a long pause, he added, "I am sure something will pop into my head here in the midst of this press conference, with all of the pressure of trying to come up with an answer, but it hadn't (sic) yet." The president went on to defend his decision to invade Afghanistan, then Iraq, and in the end did not identify a single mistake he had made. Enough said.

☐ Contextual Intelligence

Effective leaders are good diagnosticians, and good diagnosticians must develop a contextual awareness that allows them to accurately read the situation and apply the correct remedy to the problem. This *contextual intelligence* recognizes that leadership is largely contextual, and that the context or situation sets parameters.[40]

As Joseph S. Nye, Jr. has written,

Contextual intelligence allows leaders to adjust their style to the situation and to their followers' needs. It enables them to create flows of information that "educate their hunches." It involves the broad political skill of not only sizing up group politics, but understanding the positions and strengths of various stakeholders so as to decide when and how to use transactional and inspirational skills. It is the self-made part of luck. In unstructured situations, it is often more difficult to ask the right questions than to get the right answer. Leaders with contextual intelligence are skilled at providing meaning or a road map by defining the problem that a group confronts. They understand the tension between the different values involved in an issue, and how to balance the desirable with what is feasible. In particular, contextual intelligence requires an understanding of groups' cultures, the distribution of power resources, followers' needs and demands, information flows, and timing.[41]

Presidents are both weak and powerful—depending on context. A president in foreign affairs is fairly powerful; a president in domestic and economic affairs is largely constrained. Likewise, a president facing a crisis is ceded significant powers, whereas during normal or routine times, faces a myriad of roadblocks.

FDR could not have gotten his New Deal legislation passed had it not been for the crisis of the Great Depression. Lincoln could not have gotten away with suspending *habeas corpus* were it not for the Civil War. A misreading of context and what it permits (e.g., Reagan and the Iran-Contra scandal) leads to defeat, humiliation, or both.

☐ Conclusion

The end result in attempting to arrive at sound leadership is found in the work of Aristotle, who enjoined leaders to pursue phronesis. In his *Nicomanchean Ethics*, Aristotle tried to guide the leader toward effective decision making that pursued noble goals yet recognized content and its limits. Search not for a pie in the sky, but work for worthy, attainable ends here on Earth.

Effective leaders are adept generalists who exhibit skill, sound temperament, good judgment, self-awareness, and context-awareness. They are flexible and empathetic, base their lives in value and can connect with others. And effective leaders help us to adapt to necessary changes—the topic of our next chapter.

☐ Notes

1. See Ben McGrath, "Head Start: Steve Clarkson Grooms Future Quarterbacks for the Pros," *The New Yorker* (October 15, 2012): p. 39.
2. James O'Toole, *Creating the Good Life: Applying Aristotle's Wisdom to Find Meaning and Happiness* (Emmaus, PA: Rodale Books, 2005).

3. See R. E. Boyatzis, *The Competent Manager: A Model for Effective Performance* (New York, NY: Wiley, 1982); and L. M. and S. M. Spencer, *Competence at Work* (New York, NY: Wiley, 1993).
4. See Mary Ellen Joyce and William C. Adams, "Leadership Competencies," in *Political and Civic Leadership: A Reference Handbook*, Vol. 2., ed. Richard A. Couto (Los Angeles, CA: Sage, 2010), pp. 875–885.
5. Hamilton, Madison, and Jay, *The Federalist Papers*, ed. Michael A. Genovese (New York, NY: Palgrave Macmillan, 2009), p. 33.
6. Nannerl O. Keohane, "On Leadership," *Perspectives on Politics 3*, no. 4 (December 2005): p. 710.
7. Jonah Lehrer, *How We Decide* (New York, NY: Mariner Books, 2009), pp. 13 & 26.
8. See Michael Isikoff and David Corn, *Hubris: The Inside Story of Spin, Scandal, and the Selling of the Iraq War* (New York, NY: Three Rivers Press, 2006); Davis Owen, *The Hubris Syndrome: Bush, Blair, and the Intoxication of Power* (London, England: Metheun Publishing, 2011); Thomas E. Ricks, *Fiasco: The American Military Adventure in Iraq* (New York, NY: Paradigm Publishers, 2006).
9. Irving L. Janus, *Victims of Groupthink: A Psychological Study of Foreign Policy Decisions and Fiascos* (New York, NY: Houghton Mifflin, 1972).
10. President Dwight D. Eisenhower said "Organization cannot of course make a successful leader out of a dunce, any more than it should make a decision for its chief." Eisenhower, *The White House Years: Waging Peace, 1956–1961* (New York, NY: Doubleday, 1965), p. 630.
11. Balthezar Gracian, *The Art of Worldly Wisdom* (Boston, MA: Shambhala, 1993), p. 20.
12. Plutarch, *The Rise and Fall of Athens* (New York, NY: Penguin, 1960), p. 88.
13. Gracian, *The Art of Worldly Wisdom*, p. 130.
14. D. Wechsler, *The Measurement and Appraisal of Adult Intelligence* (Baltimore, MD: Williams and Wilkins, 1958).
15. E. L. Thorndike, "Intelligence and Its Uses," *Harpers Magazine 140* (1920): pp. 227–235.
16. Peter Salovey and John D. Mayer, "Emotional Intelligence," in *Imagination, Cognition, and Personality* (Amityville, NY: Baywood, 1990), pp. 185–211. Quotes on pp. 190 and 202.
17. See Daniel Goleman, *Working with Emotional Intelligence* (New York, NY: Bantam Books, 1998); and Davis Caruso and Peter Salovey, *The Emotionally Intelligent Manager* (Hoboken, NJ: Jossey-Bass, 2004).
18. Aristotle, *The Nicomachean Ethics*.
19. Daniel Goleman, "What Makes a Leader?," *Harvard Business Review* (January 2004).
20. Attributed to Aristotle by Will Durant, *The Story of Philosophy* (New York, NY: Pocket Books, 1991).
21. Atul Gawande, "Personal Best: Top Athletes and Singers Have Coaches. Should You?," *The New Yorker* (October 3, 2011).

22. Dev Patnaik, *Wired to Care: How Companies Prosper When They Create Widespread Empathy* (Upper Saddle River, NJ: FT Press, 2009).
23. Quoted in Anthony Everitt, *Cicero: The Life and Times of Rome's Greatest Politician* (New York, NY: Random House, 2001), p. 163.
24. Sun Tzu, *The Art of War* (Boston, MA: Shambhala, 1993), p. 49.
25. Warren F. Kimball, *The Juggler: Franklin Roosevelt as a Wartime Statesman* (Princeton, NJ: Princeton University Press, 1994), p. 7.
26. Richard Carlson, *Don't Sweat the Small Stuff* (New York, NY: Hyperion, 1997).
27. See *The Bhagavad Gita*, part of the *Mahabharata*, on ancient Indian epic poem.
28. See Michael A. Genovese, *The Nixon Presidency: Power and Politics in Turbulent Times* (New York, NY: Greenwood Press, 1990), and *The Watergate Crises* (New York, NY: Greenwood Press, 1999).
29. Michael A. Genovese and Iwan Morgan, *Watergate Remembered: The Legacy for American Politics* (New York, NY: Palgrave Macmillan, 2012).
30. Warren Bennis, *On Becoming a Leader* (New York, NY: Perseus, 2009).
31. See, for example, John Adair, *The Leadership of Muhammad* (London, England: Kogan Pages, 2010); and Joseph A. Kechichian and R. Hrair Dekmejian, *The Just Prince: A Manual of Leadership* (London, England: Sagi Books, 2003).
32. Robert I. Sutton, *The No Asshole Rule: Building a Civilized Workplace and Surviving One That Isn't* (New York, NY: Business Plus, 2010).
33. Robert Greene, *48 Laws of Power* (New York, NY: Penguin, 2000).
34. Father Theodore Hesburgh, former president, Notre Dame University. *Time*, May 1987.
35. T. E. Lawrence, *The Seven Pillars of Wisdom* (Radford, VA: Wilder Publications, 2011).
36. Ron Heifetz, *Leadership Without Easy Answers* (Cambridge, MA: Harvard University Press, 1998), and *The Practice of Adaptive Leadership* (Cambridge, MA: Harvard Business Press, 2009).
37. Alina Tugend, *Better By Mistake* (New York, NY: Riverhead Books, 2011).
38. Gerald R. Ford, *A Time to Heal* (New York, NY: Berkeley Books, 1979), p. 183.
39. Quoted in Yamamoto Tsunetomo, *Hagakure: The Book of the Samurai* (Boston, MA: Shambhala, 1979), p. 42
40. Joseph Nye, *The Powers to Lead* (New York, NY: Oxford University Press, 2008).
41. Joseph S. Nye, Jr., *Presidential Leadership and the Creation of the American Era* (Princeton, NJ: Princeton University Press, 2013), pp. 13–14.

Leadership and the Crosscurrents of Change

> I am well aware that the moment of any great change . . . is unavoidably the moment of terror and confusion. The mind, highly agitated by hope, suspicion, and apprehension, continues without rest till the change be accomplished.
> —Thomas Paine, Letter to the People of France, 1792

> **Genovese Leadership Theorem:** In politics, the lesser of two evils usually wins over the evil of two lesser, and vice versa.

Individuals as well as organizations often resist change. Even when things are not going well, we tend to stick with what is familiar rather than risk venturing into uncharted territory. The comfort of the known usually trumps the uncertainty of the new and untested.

Anyone who doubts this need look no further than the failure of Israel and the Palestinians to abandon "tried and untrue" methods—politics as (un)usual—and attempt some new approach to achieving peace. Their current security dilemma is evidence that Albert Einstein was correct when he defined *insanity* as "doing the same thing over and over again and expecting different results."

Yet why should we be so? Individuals are said to be rational and organizations/states seek to survive and thrive.[1] Why is change so difficult even in the face of repeated failure or disappointment?

As W. H. Auden noted:

> We would rather be ruined than changed,
> We would rather die in our dread
> Than climb the cross of the moment
> And let our illusions die.[2]

Although essentially true, such sentiments can also be powerfully dysfunctional. They inhibit personal development and organizational survival. There is an old Yiddish proverb that says, "The only person who likes change is a wet baby." But change is necessary. It is a part of the grand cycle of life. As Emerson reminded us, "Society acquires new arts, and loses old instincts." And as Marcus Aurelius wrote in Book VII (1993, 139), No. 18, of his *Meditations*,

> Is anyone afraid of change? Why, what can take place without change? What then is more pleasing or more suitable to the universal nature? And can you take a bath unless the wood undergoes a change? And can you be nourished, unless the food undergoes a change? And can anything else that is useful be accomplished without change?

If change were easy and simple, we would likely see more of our goals realized. But change can be difficult and painful, sometimes we avoid it like the plague. It is easier *not* to change; easier, but what happens when change is necessary?

Change is as difficult for organizations as it is for individuals. Few established organizations are innovation-friendly, yet many try to be. Why do we feel so threatened by change?

☐ Was Machiavelli Right?

Change is disruptive. We are familiar with the often quoted excerpt from *The Prince*:

> And it must be considered that nothing is more difficult to transact nor more dubious to succeed, nor more dangerous to manage, than to make oneself first to introduce new orders. Because the introducer has for enemies all those whom the old orders benefit, and has for lukewarm defenders all those who might benefit by the new orders. Which lukewarmness springs in part from the incredulity of men, who do not truly believe in new things if they do not see solid experience born of them.[3]

New methods threaten old orders. Reward systems change, power relations are altered, new skills must be developed. Our comfort zones are threatened by change. We fear what might lurk around the corner, so we stay where we are. Better the devil you know than the devil you don't.

We have already discussed the key role leaders play in promoting change and in helping organizations adapt to needed change. But before leaders can employ adaptive strategies, they must prepare the organization for change. We know that change must come. How do we bend that change in desired directions? And although leaders can be key, a variety of forces are involved in the change process. And this process—and we need to think of change as a *process*—involves a variety of actors. Political scientist John Kingdom calls our attention to the "pattern of events" that leaders can help manage: "Leaders," Kingdom argues, "are like surfers waiting for the big wave. Individuals do not control waves, but can ride them. Individuals do not control events or structures, but can anticipate them and bend them to their purpose to some degree."[4] And Tom Cronin and I have characterized the change process as best understood resembling a three-act play. In Act I, new ideas are formulated and presented. In Act II, these ideas begin to attract a following. In Act III, leaders finally get involved, overseeing their enactment and implementation. Note that leaders only get actively involved at the end of the process.[5]

In trying to creatively manage the change process, we must answer a series of questions related to change:

> Why do we need to change? What is *wrong*?
> What happens if we do not change?
> Where do we wish to go? What is *our vision*?
> Do we need major surgery or minor tinkering?
> Will reform, deform?
> How will these changes reinforce our core values?
> How might the *laws of unintended consequences* lead us in undesirable directions?
> How can we enlist elite and mass support for change?
> What does a cost-benefit analysis tell us?
> Have we explored all our options?
> Is our decision-making process evidence based?
> How do we truly listen to—and perhaps learn from—our critics?
> Can in-house *devil's advocates* help us avoid mistakes?
> What are the roadblocks to change?
> What are the key pathways to change?
> How do we grease the wheels of the change process?
> Will *backward mapping* (starting at a desired destination, then moving backward on our path of change) enlighten our task?
> How can we foster a change climate (fear or hope)?
> How best to frame the case for change?

Today, change occurs more rapidly than ever before.[6] No sooner do you buy the iPad than the iPad 2 comes out. As soon as you buy your HDTV, 3D comes along. The ability to adapt to all these changes is the key to survival and growth, both individually and organizationally. So how does one get the wind to blow into the sails of change?

Both internal and external factors from expected and unexpected sources can trigger change. New technologies, shifts in power, economic changes, natural and man-made disasters, etc. all can drive change.

Nations, organizations, and individuals face several particularly vexing challenges. There is the *surprise crisis* (something sprung on you unexpectedly, e.g., the 9/11 attack against the United States); the *expected crisis* (something you know is coming but for some reason cannot head off—e.g., the debt crisis in the United States or a major hurricane); and there are the *expected/surprise crises* (you know it is coming, but when it comes, you have no early warning—e.g., the upcoming massive earthquake in California).

Each of these crises requires a response, and each requires change; some in reaction to the surprise, others in anticipation of the event. We can't be ready for everything, but we *should* be ready for expected surprises. In reaction to a surprise crisis, we react, we change, we adapt, we adjust. In response to expected crises, we plan, we prepare, we change now for the crisis that will come later.

In terms of leadership, a gradual crisis is often more difficult to deal with than a sudden crisis. In a sudden crisis such as 9/11, the system is dealt a quick, surprise blow. We often react emotionally, *demanding* that the leader save us. In the case of President Bush, 9/11 freed him and empowered him. He was largely free of the constraining chains of the separation of powers system and was empowered to act—on his own—as what Clinton Rossiter has called a "constitutional dictator."[7]

However, a gradual crisis offers no such opportunity to use power. They meet with resistance as the normal checks and balances are fully operational, as there is no widespread recognition that the government must act quickly. The U.S. debt crisis and the climate crisis are such gradually approaching crises.

The gradually approaching crisis, on the other hand, may be (1) more difficult to see as it slowly creeps ahead, and (2) rejected by those who have a significant stake in the status quo, and (3) subject to doubt and controversy about the impending doom. The global climate change crisis is just such a gradually approaching crisis.

Some deny the science behind the claims of a coming crisis, others see a chicken little crying that the sky is falling, still others have a vested financial or political stake in the status quo. To deal with such a crisis, a *sense of urgency* must be established. And yet our leaders have failed to enlighten us, and we lurch—slowly but inextricably—toward disaster.

In individuals, change triggers a set of predictable stressors: anxiety, confusion, fear, frustration, and anger; our basic defense mechanisms take over often mimicking the stages associated with the Kubler-Ross Stages of Grief: denial, anger, bargaining, depression, and acceptance. Or we may overpersonalize. When the leader calls for change, some listeners hear that they are no longer valued.

Change on an individual level can be difficult and require a reversing of the brain. Our brains are wired to the status quo. What we have done repeatedly in the past is what the brain is biased toward. Our brains become wired to a default position that is directed toward what we know, what we have done, what our brains have become accustomed to. To change, new wiring is required, and that rewiring can only come about through repetition until repetition becomes habit and our brains forge new connections, new pathways, new wiring. We must "create new neural pathways in the brain." As Kevin Hogan writes,

> The status quo is the status quo for just this reason. That which is familiar is the path of least resistance. This is also why the brain reacts so strongly with a negative response to all but the most familiar requests or behaviors. It takes enormous initial effort to change because one literally must forge new highways in the brain. Once formed, the highways must be strengthened through regular usage and maintained by even further usage.[8]

This takes a great deal of energy, and as our brains are mostly gluttonous consumers of energy, the brain resists. The easiest way to get someone to change—a secret the military and religious cults have known for years—is to totally change one's frame of reference or one's environment. Strip a person down and rebuild him. Yet how often can we do this?

And yet leaders, organizations, and states in Machiavelli's time as in ours, know that while threatening, change is necessary, inevitable, and often worthwhile. How then, do we pave the way for constructive, intentional change?

☐ The Occasional Attraction of Change

In stable societies, when things are going well, where problems seem small and life seems good, leadership is largely unnecessary. In such cases, what is most needed is effective management.[9] But when clashes occur, when society must change, adjust, adapt, when choices must be made, leadership becomes necessary.

Although change is difficult, there are times when change is seen as an attractive, even necessary, alternative to maintaining the status quo. In troubled times, we are often willing to entertain fundamental, even radical change in hopes that major surgery will cure what ails us. Dissatisfaction thus may open the door to possible change and is the predicate of abandoning the status quo.

When things go wrong, we are often willing and anxious to change course. A business losing a significant portion of market share, a political system in the throes of voter discontent, an individual facing debilitating disease all lead to the search for a better way.

However, in especially hard times, demagogues may emerge promising salvation, and at such times, they may indeed draw a significant following. A radical message that would be dismissed in peaceful times may resonate in troubling times.

☐ Leadership's Adaptive Function

I am very ecumenical about leadership. Thus, I do not subscribe to one, narrow model of leadership for all seasons. Worshiping the false god of a single leadership model is narrow, confining, and usually wrong. The tough-as-nails approach of Jack Welch may be useful for one situation, but at other times, the Servant Leadership model fits the needs of the situation.

The first task of the leader is to be a *diagnostician*: You must accurately read the situation and discern just what is wrong. Next, the effective leader is good at *prescribing* a cure for the sick patient. Then, the leader must be a *technician*, able to devise a workable means to cure the illness. While doing this, the effective leader must also be a *military commander*, devising a broad strategy for success and insuring adherence to the strategy. Also, the leader must be a *cheerleader*, able to rally the troops to action. Of course, the leader must be a *guru*, inspiring others with a vision for accomplishment. Then, the leader must be a *manager*, insuring that the plan of change is well implemented. Let us not forget that the effective leader then must be an *evaluator*, able to see if the original strategy was the correct one. All the while, the leader must be a *psychiatrist*, able to delve into the inner workings of him- or herself, the organization, and the clientele group. And at times, the leader must be a *revolutionary*, who destroys old orders and creates new ones.

One leadership model cannot account for all these varied roles played out by one person, the leader. And this is why leadership is difficult, yet also very important. Adhering to a single model of leadership may be right now and then—after all, as we all know, a broken clock tells the right time twice a day—yet what we want, and what we need, is not to be right now and then, but to be right almost all the time.

All organizations, all institutions, must adapt. Adaptation requires change. Leaders help us make the necessary adaptions that must be made.[10]

Leaders inevitably serve as both unifiers and dividers. Effective leaders find ways to balance the two. Yes, we want our leaders to bring us together as a nation, organization, or community. And yet, leadership is also about choice, and in choosing, some win and others lose. A sensitive leader discerns when to compromise, when to go for it all, when to bring people together, and when to sharpen division and choose. A bit of conflict can be a healthy thing; too much conflict can lead to open warfare. Leaders have to be both movers and shakers.

Although *ideological leaders* often excite the passions of followers, most are too rigid or close-minded to govern efficiently over the long haul. The most effective leaders, like Augustus (Rome, 63BC–14AD) were able to temper their strongly held beliefs and practice a brand of *pragmatism* that helped attain balance and stability. Augustus, for example, firmly believed that public aid to the poor in the form of social welfare, or the dole, made people lazy and dependent on the state. Yet he did not try to wean the poor off of welfare, fearing that such changes might stir the embers of class warfare and lead to instability.

☐ Our Rational Brain Confronts Change

Our rational brain knows that change is inevitable, often beneficial, at times necessary, yet we are more than our rational selves. We also have emotions, and emotions play an indispensable role in decision making. Our *bounded rationality* means we decide with the head and the heart.

The rational brain and the emotional brain are not necessarily in conflict. In fact, they can and should be mutually supportive, as Jonah Lehrer writes, "making good decisions requires us to use both sides of the mind."[11]

We are complex, contradictory, paradoxical beings, often our own worst enemies. We are pulled in different directions, unsure of which way to go. This is natural and inevitable. As Walt Whitman wrote in his poem "Song of Myself," "Do I contradict myself? Very well then I contradict myself. I am large, I contain multitudes." Although this complexity can paralyze us, we must find ways to embrace complexity and deal constructively with the contradictions in ourselves and in life.

Our brains have essentially two modes of thinking/deciding: fast and slow,[12] or relying on an "automatic system" or a "reflective system."[13] The fast or automatic method "operates quickly, effortlessly, subconsciously." The slow or reflective system is "driven not by raw sensation but by logic and reason."[14] The brain, in an effort to save energy, pushes us to think fast, automatically. Wisdom tells us that whenever possible, we should think slowly and reflectively.

The leader must help us adapt to and accept needed change. But how can the leader him- or herself come to grips with change? In order to make rational decisions about change, the leader must think clearly about change. And yet, the normal functioning of the brain may not lend itself to comprehensive thinking. What is the leader to do?

In all complex decision scenarios, the leader must "think about thinking." Usually referred to as metacognition, it involves examining and monitoring how we think, process, and use information, and how we understand the process of deciding. J. H. Flavell, believed to be the first person to use the term, defined metacognition as "one's knowledge concerning one's own cognitive processes."[15]

Even if we are rational, the context in which we make decisions may prevent us from deciding rationally. After all, we usually lack sufficient information; we are limited by time (and our own impatience); and our brains are naturally drawn to shortcuts in decision making. This decision-making dilemma is referred to as *bounded rationality*.

We easily and often fall into traps. Our brains are greedy energy users and search for shortcuts in making decisions. Too often we rely on *heuristics*, or mental rules of thumb as shortcuts to make decision making easier for us. Although we should think deeply and thoroughly, we often jump to conclusions based on already stored up knowledge, or fall back on biases and assumptions. This may lead us to make errors in judgment.

Leaders simply do not have the luxury of making very many mistakes. Therefore—especially in the ambiguous and uncomfortable world of change—the leader must not rely on heuristics but must constantly think about the process of thinking. Only then do we have a chance of rising above the shortcuts our brains want us to take.

How can a leader help us make intelligent decisions about change? After all, change triggers powerful emotions. These emotions, when they take over our decision-making process, can lead to irrational or self-destructive outcomes.

Change is persuasion. The leader must persuade the organization of the need for change and of the change they need. Yet if we are usually unreceptive to appeals for change, how can a leader bring us on board? Leaders must remember that to persuade, appeals must be made both to reason and emotion. Information alone does not move us. As thinking and feeling beings, we need to be rationally persuaded *and* emotionally moved.

"Intelligence," John Holt asserts, "is not the measure of how much we know how to do, but of how we behave when we don't know what to do."[16] The leader must help us through the maze by defining reality; giving it meaning; setting a clear and compelling course; openly acknowledging the fear and uncertainty people feel, inspire and reassure; and move the organization. The narrative matters.

☐ The Organization/State Confronts Change

How does a leader get the organization to make the changes believed necessary for growth of survival? How does the organization achieve significant buy in for change?

Organizations can be rigid. Their cultures developed over many years and often seem intractable. Participants know the ground rules. They are comfortable repeating familiar patterns of behavior. The change agent often feels like Sysiphus.

Change can happen when:

1. There is widespread recognition that the status quo is unacceptable.
2. The leader can create a sense of urgency.
3. The machinery of the organization is altered.
4. The leader can lead people through the change process.

In this way, the leader's role in achieving change is essential. He or she must (1) be an accurate diagnostician of the problem; (2) be an advocate for change; (3) supply purpose and direction; (4) reassure and communicate hope; (5) acknowledge the fears that change generates; (6) provide a roadmap for the future; (7) reincentivize the organization by changing the reward or punishment mechanism; (8) align the organization resources and actions with the desired direction of change; (9) change people's behavior; (10) get the right people in the right places; and (11) ensure that those wishing to thwart change fear taking you on.

It is a long and intimidating list. So much must go the right way if change is to be achieved. That is why roughly 75 percent of CEOs questioned, believe their efforts at organizational change had failed. And often their change efforts resulted in unintended and negative consequences.[17]

☐ The Success of Failure

As previously noted, most efforts at change fail, some miserably. And yet, failure is a common, even essential ingredient to change.

Any review of the biographies of great inventors, powerful corporate executives, or public leaders reveals a pattern of frequent, even repeated failure, before achieving success. What distinguishes the successful failure from the failed failure? A three-part pattern seems operative in virtually all cases. The successful failure will:

1. Take responsibility for failure
2. Be open to the lessons failure teaches us
3. Persist

Individuals and organizations must be mindful of the persistence of failure while also committing to trying and trying again.

Change requires the unfreezing, changing, then refreezing of accepted practices.[18] The unfreezing phase is often the most difficult. Absent an external crisis, we are prone to avoid risking even necessary change. Leading change thus requires a change process. As described by John Kotter, this process involves eight steps:

1. Create/Establish a sense of urgency.
2. Form a coalition or team for change.
3. Offer an attractive vision.
4. Use multiple outlets to communicate this vision.
5. Empower others to enact the vision.
6. Create short-term wins to build confidence in change.
7. Consolidate change and make more change.
8. Institutionalize (refreeze) the change.[19]

☐ Back to the Future: The Conservative Principles of Organizational Change

As the renowned community organizer Saul Alinsky noted, "Men don't like to step abruptly out of the security of familiar experience:

They need a bridge to cross from their own experience to a new way."[20] It is the job of creative and adaptive leadership to point the way, to help followers envision that bridge that can be crossed, to ease some of the anxiety about necessary change.

Change takes people out of their comfort zones. New is scary. That is why, whenever possible, change should be couched in conservative principles. The narrative matters, and a leader who can convince people that the change ahead is really a reclaiming of a known past may pave the way for change. The comfort of the past may be employed to ease the fear of the future change.

The picture (or vision) a leader paints gives people a clearer sense of destination. This picture tells a story: the narrative. This narrative shapes our sense of reality, it defines reality for us.

A leader presents a vision through a narrative that refers to the past and convinces us to reclaim our past; asks us to go back to the known, the secure, the tried and true; and creates a pathway for change. We need not fear the future, or recoil from unknown, but go forward/back to what is true and tested.

Change and the future are not our enemies, they are our fellow travelers, our heritage, our history, and our tomorrow. The future is thus not unknown, but a revitalization of our truest selves. For example, when Martin Luther King, Jr., John F. Kennedy, and Lyndon B. Johnson called for civil rights change, they often did so by insisting that equality was part of the DNA of America, that a part of society was denied these fundamental rights, that we trace to the framers ("We hold these truths to be self-evident that all men are created equal") was cause to go back to the first principles and correct an operational flaw in our original grand design. This was not new—this was making sure old traditions were fully guaranteed. Civil rights reform thus meant going back to the future.

☐ Conclusion

If the organization is to survive, it must embrace, or at a minimum, tolerate change. Change or die. If an individual is to survive, he or she must adapt and change. Yet change can be frightening, and the individual and the organization will resist. To be effective, the leader must find ways to overcome the inevitable blowback that efforts at change will elicit.

Leaders must be change agents. Often they will strategically cloak their actions in conservative rhetoric, but they must pave the way for the changes necessary for survival and growth.

☐ Notes

1. I use organization and state interchangeably, following Jay who argues that they are essentially the same organism. See A. Jay, *Management and Machiavelli* (London, England: Hodden and Stoughton, 1967).
2. W. H. Auden, "The Age of Anxiety," 1948 (this poem won the Pulitzer Prize).
3. Niccolo Machiavelli, *The Prince*, trans. and ed. Angelo M. Cordevilla (New Haven, CT: Yale University Press, 1997), Chapter 6, p. 22.
4. John Kingdom, *Agendas, Alternatives, and Public Policies*, 2nd ed. (New York, NY: Longman, 2003), pp. 224–226.
5. Thomas E. Cronin and Michael A. Genovese, *Leadership Matters: Unleashing the Power of Paradox* (Boulder, CO: Paradigm Publishers, 2012), pp. 185–194.
6. P. C. Nutt, "De-development as a Way to Change Contemporary Organizations," in *Research in Organizational Change and Development*, ed. R. W. Woodman and W. A. Pasmore (Oxford, England: Elsevier, 2001), pp. 81–115.
7. Clinton Rossiter, *Constitutional Dictatorship: Crisis Government in the Modern Democracies* (New Brunswick, NJ: Transaction Publishers, 2002).
8. Kevin Hogan, *The Science of Influence* (Hoboken, NJ: Wiley, 2011), pp. 2–3.
9. Peter F. Drucker, "What Makes an Effective Executive," *Harvard Business Review* (June 2004).
10. Ron Heifetz, A. Grashow, and M. Linksy, *The Practice of Adaptive Leadership* (Boston, MA: Harvard Business Press, 2009).
11. Jonah Lehrer, *How We Decide* (Boston, MA: Mariner Books, 2009) p. xvi.
12. See Daniel Kahneman, *Thinking Fast and Slow* (New York, NY: Farrar, Strauss and Giroux, 2011).
13. See Sheena Iyengar, *The Art of Choosing* (New York, NY: Twelve, 2010).
14. Ibid., pp. 114–115.
15. J. H. Flavell, "Metacognition Aspects of Problem Solving," in *The Nature of Intelligence*, ed. L. B. Resnick (Hillsdale, NJ: Erlbaum, 1976), p. 232.
16. John Holt, *Teach Your Own* (New York, NY: Delacourt, 1981).
17. Margaret J. Wheatley and Myron Kellner-Rogers, "Bringing Life to Organizational Change," *Journal for Strategic Performance Measurement* (April/May 1998).
18. Adapted from Kurt Lewin, *Resolving Social Conflicts and Field Theory in Social Science* (Washington, D.C.: American Psychological Association, 1997).
19. Adapted from John Kotter, *Leading Change* (Cambridge, MA: Harvard Business Press, 1996).
20. Saul D. Alinsky, *Rules for Radicals* (New York, NY: Vintage Books, 1971), p. xxi

Building Leaders

The Genovese Leadership Academy

"A leader is a dealer in hope."
—Napoleon Bonaparte

Genovese Leadership Theorem: As my mother said, "You can catch more flies with honey than with vinegar." (But why would you want to catch flies? I ask!)

Welcome to the Genovese Leadership Academy, your place for one-stop shopping for all your leadership needs. While here, you'll "learn what you need to learn" about becoming an effective leader.

If we could construct a training program for would-be leaders, what would it look like, what would it include? The short answer is: Start with an excellent and wide-ranging liberal arts education, then read, read, read, then practice, practice, practice.

The leadership training program contains three core tracks: (1) a classical liberal arts background; (2) the lives of the great and good; and (3) the essentials of leadership.

☐ Liberal Arts as Your Starting Point

We live in a super-connected world, a world of rapid, and often surprising change. This world requires flexibility, puzzle solving, and highly transferable skills. Virtually everything you think you know today will likely be obsolete tomorrow. Welcome to the world of hyper-change. Do not sit back and get comfortable or you will be left behind.

To stay afloat in such a world, you will need to be a lifelong learner. You have to know how to know, and learn how to learn.

The skills you will have to master will evolve and change in a matter of nanoseconds. And once you've mastered them, you will have to learn how to deal with new issues, new technologies, new challenges. School isn't over—it is just beginning. Gone are the days when you could master one skill and be set for life.

Imagine it this way, the job you will do for most of your life has not even been invented yet. What can possibly prepare one for such a world? Why, the classic liberal arts, of course.

At its best, the liberal arts educates one to be a lifelong learner, an intelligent generalist, an effective synthesizer, a critical thinker, a creative person, with an integrative mind that can make connections across disciplines and creatively confront new and different challenges.

It is believed that the Roman orator and statesman (and a bit of a polymath himself—Marcus Tillius), Cicero, was the first person to use the phrase, *liberal arts education*. He saw it as something that had two goals: the search for truth (an individual's personal journey) and the creation of the enlightened public citizen (a civic duty). In combining the private with the public, Cicero envisioned education as an endeavor that would not only serve the needs of the individual to grow and search for truth, but also have a public or communal purpose to help improve the polis.[1]

Joanne B. Ciulla puts leadership into a liberal arts context when she writes:

> People often think of leadership school as some sort of training program. Yet when you think of it, the very idea of leadership *training* is an oxymoron. Training implies development of a skill in conformity to certain practices and procedures. Leadership would seem to be the opposite of this. While leadership requires certain skills, I am not so sure leadership itself is a skill. If anything, leadership is more about initiative, perspective, imagination, morality, and the ability to think well and understand people and the world around us. Ideally, a liberal arts education provides the foundation for leadership and life in human society.[2]

Today, a liberal arts education is the starting point in the leader's more formal academic training. A liberal arts education is a broad-based, rigorous training in a wide range of academic fields. It is—and must be—inter- and multidisciplinary and integrative of many different disciplines. In the classroom it includes, among other things, education in classics, literature (especially Shakespeare), philosophy, theology, politics, history, ethics, economics, communication (oral and written), decision making, organizational behavior, and psychology.

Such an education teaches one to be familiar and comfortable with the world of ideas. It teaches one to become a puzzle solver and a connector of dots. It gives one the ability to apply the methods and knowledge drawn from a variety of fields and direct it to problem solving. Its courses might include: the future 101, cross cultural inquiry, critical thinking, logic and reason, debate, the scientific method, social justice, thinking out of the box, the change process, democracy, race and gender, dealing with diversity, or globalization.

The liberal arts puts the higher into higher education. It is an invitation to engage in the great debates and questions that have vexed humankind for centuries. It allows us to converse and argue with the greatest minds of all time: Plato, Aristotle, Aquinas, and Marx.

The liberal arts compels us to understand what was and what is, and imagine what might be. It teaches us habits of the mind that liberate us from prejudice and narrowness. They help us intellectually integrate the many points into a coherent whole. They are multidisciplinary, and they are discipline benders. They help us connect the dots. They help us deal with uncertainty. The liberal arts teach us to "know thyself." The liberal arts teaches us to be intelligent generalists.

Being an intelligent generalist allows the leader to spread his net widely and grasp the interconnectedness of several seemingly disparate fields and become a synthesizer who can connect and integrate a wide range of information.

As Howard Gardner notes, effective leaders are able to draw connections, bring ideas from different sources together. He writes: "As synthesizers, they will need to be able to gather together information from disparate sources and put it all together in ways that work for themselves and can be communicated to other persons."[3]

☐ The Lives of the Great and Good

We can greatly profit from a method of learning that has a long and rich tradition. I refer here to the disciplined and purposeful reading of the lives of the great and good who have preceded us. From these life stories, we can generate models (both positive and negative) of behavior we may wish to emulate or avoid.[4]

Where to start? With the classics, of course. And there is no better place to begin than with Plutarch (of Chaeronea). Born in 46 AD, Plutarch set out to write biographies describing some of the most powerful leaders of Athens and Rome, and to directly compare leaders who face comparable challenges. His *Life of Theseus* and *Life of Romulus*, compares the founders of Athens and Rome, and his *Life of Alexander* and *Life of Caesar*, two great conquerors. His goal was not to write traditional histories, but to examine lives. Plutarch puts great stock in judgment and character. He holds up the parallel lives to scrutiny, offering a wealth of material from which we may judge what it is that constitutes a good leader.

Niccolo Machiavelli (1469–1527), Florentine diplomat, statesman, historian, military strategist, philosopher, and polymath, like Plutarch before him, carefully examined the lives of leaders and generals to discern what constituted greatness, and how a leader might emulate great leaders like Moses or Castruccio Castracani (of Lucca, Italy). In *The Prince* (a book often misunderstood by critics), Machiavelli rejects Christian idealism in favor of blunt realism, and gives his prince advice, not on how to be a good person, but how to be an effective leader and wielder of power.

Machiavelli's composite leader (as mentioned earlier) was one who appeared virtuous, was feared or loved but never hated by the people, gained the support of the people, effectively used force, exercised strategic boldness, and demonstrated sound judgment based on an accurate reading of the situation.

It is not the ancients alone that we can look for guidance. Modern biographies of corporate stars (often self-serving yet still valuable), bios of people like Nelson Mandela, Andrai Sakharov, Martin Luther King Jr., both Roosevelts, Lincoln, and others can bring ancient wisdom and questions into a modern context.

☐ The Essentials of Leadership

We have already spent much time dissecting the essential skills of leadership (Chapter 3), so we can be brief here. Essentially what we must do here is draw closer connections between a liberal arts education and leadership development.

If one begins with a rigorous, broad-based liberal arts education, adds to that the in-depth reading and reflection on the lives and characters of prominent, powerful, and successful leaders of the past, then systematically engages in a deliberative practice of leadership development, one can graduate, as it were, from our leadership academy and be prepared to confront the challenge of twenty-first century leadership.

The conscientious student of leadership can start his or her leadership life in a variety of constructive ways. While in college, opportunities for deliberative practice in leadership development abound. Beyond the liberal arts education touted above, students should strongly consider study abroad (especially in a non-English speaking country). Nothing during your college years will likely be more transformative than studying abroad. You stretch yourself, challenge your comfort zone, learn about other cultures and ways of being, and—if one reflects deeply about the experience—grow more as a result of studying abroad than just about anything you can do in college.

Also, internships can be very valuable, as can joining the debate team, writing for the school newspaper, engaging in sustained service, even taking speech and acting classes.

After college, community organizing, a year or two of public service (such as Teach for America) or working in the inner city, can help one fine-tune the nascent leadership skills envisioned in college.

Finding mentors and coaches is an often overlooked, yet essential step in the road to leadership. You would be amazed how often very busy people will take the time to mentor young talent. Do not be shy about seeking out mentors. You can learn from the victories and the successes, as well as the setbacks and failures, of others, become educated about a particular field, see how someone confronts challenges, manages their time, how their mind works, how they solve real-world problems, etc. Then, in twenty years, you too can serve as a mentor to others.

By contentiously, systematically, and deliberatively working to fine-tune your natural talent; by nurturing habits of leadership; by embracing a liberal arts education; by reading the masters on the lives of the great and good; and by working to develop your leadership toolkit, you can become a measurably better leader. One may not become a Mount Rushmore leader, but with training and practice, one can certainly become a much more effective leader. And while Machiavelli reminds us in *The Prince*, fortune or luck plays a role, and there are some things over which we have little or no control, it behooves us to make the most and the best of what we have. Leadership rarely just happens. It should be nurtured and developed. And there is no mystery in how this is done.

☐ Life's Lessons

I graduated from the University of Southern California. My father graduated from the College of Hard Knocks. Which of us was better prepared for life? You guessed it—dad.

Life *can* be a great teacher, if we are prepared to learn its lessons. Experience matters. Derek Jeter, New York Yankee All Star shortstop, fields hundreds of ground balls every day. He does so because come game time, he needs to have "seen it all" and be ready for any bad hop or pressure situation, armed with an extensive body of experience that prepares him to perform at peak level.

Living life fully, experiencing much, taking calculated risks, testing yourself in new and uncomfortable situations, and learning new things, all add to your leadership toolkit. Leadership is not for stay-at-home wallflowers. You have to put yourself on the line, and when out there, it helps to have experienced, reflected upon, and learned from past experiences.

☐ Leadership in/of Committees

As a college professor, I serve on what seems like 8,342 committees, which meet thirty-seven hours each day, eleven days per week. And although the burden seems onerous, it must be admitted, a tremendous number of important decisions in all organizations are made in and by committees.

Most of us hate committees. They take up lots of time and often waste time; we sit around and listen to big-mouthed babblers who just won't stop talking. Our end decisions are often watered-down to mere platitudes, and in the end, next to nothing is accomplished.

But let's rethink this bias. Yes, committee meetings are all the terrible things already mentioned, yet they *can be* places where creative leadership can shift the balance to solve important problems. The key is *purposeful committee leadership*.

How would a polymath leader approach the typical committee assignment?

- Offer to serve as chair.
- Get there first and be prepared.
- Always offer to write the first draft.
- *Frame* all issues by offering your own perspective on the issue before anyone else.
- Follow up the *framing* by turning next to an ally who will reinforce your view.
- Head off the wise guy who sits back telling *you* what *you* must do by announcing at the first meeting: I am open to any and all ideas, but know that if you make a recommendation I will immediately appoint you head of a subcommittee to report on this idea at our next meeting.

- Use the agenda as a tool of influence.
- At the end of each meeting, announce an *Action Plan* assigning who does what and who reports at the next meeting.
- Repeat at every meeting, the reason why *you* are there is to make positive change happen!

☐ Mentors and Role Models

Busy people are usually the most willing to help you. Seek out mentoring people who are already doing the things you hope one day to do—and learn from them. Busy, successful people (most of them, at least) are the most willing to give back by helping others. Find that mentor—and don't be shy about asking for help, we've all needed help along the way.

If you can't or don't find a good mentor, look to role models and learn from their experience. Read the biographies of leaders, business executives, coaches, and others. Absorb the lessons of their successes and failures. Read the great novels so that you can learn from the mistakes of others.

☐ Conclusion

Preparation, temperament, opportunity, and drive all play a significant role in your quest to be a polymath leader. And remember, so does failure. The great books and the lives of the great and good can only teach you so much. In the end, you will have to take the plunge. And although it can be scary, it can also be amazingly rewarding.

To right a wrong, improve a social condition, make the lives of people in your community better . . . to serve others. It is a recipe for a full and challenging life.

The Gold Standard—Leadership Academy Essential Reading List

Bennis, Warren, *On Becoming a Leader*
Burns, James MacGregor, *Leadership*
Gardner, John W. *On Leadership*
Machiavelli, Niccolo, *The Prince*
Hamilton, Madison, Jay, *The Federalist Papers*

Fisher and Ury, *Getting to Yes*
Finzel, Hans, *The Top Ten Mistakes Leaders Make*
Wren, Thomas, *The Leaders Companion*
Tuchman, Barbara, *The March of Folly*
Miroff, Bruce, *Icons of Democracy*
Westin, Drew, *The Political Brain*
Lehrer, Jonah, *How We Decide*
Genovese, Michael, *Memo to a New President*
Albrion, Mitch, *Tuesdays with Morrie*
Mandela, Nelson, *Long Walk to Freedom*
Caro, Robert, *The Power Broker*
Goleman, Daniel, *Emotional Intelligence*
Cronin and Genovese, *Leadership Matters*
Drucker, Peter, *The Essential Drucker; The Effective Executive*
Ibsen, Henrik, *An Enemy of the People*
Woodruff, Paul, *Reverence*
Wooden, John, *Wooden on Leadership*
Hesse, Herman, *The Journey to the East*
Lee, Harper, *To Kill a Mockingbird*
Naim, Moises, *The End of Power*
Nye, Joseph, *The Powers to Lead*

☐ Notes

1. See J. Thomas Wren, "Reinventing the Liberal Arts through Leadership," in *Leadership and the Liberal Arts*, ed. J. Thomas Wren, Ronald E. Riggio, and Michael A. Genovese (New York, NY: Palgrave Macmillan, 2009), pp. 13–36.
2. Joanne B. Ciulla, "The Jepson School: Liberal Arts as Leadership Studies," in *Leadership Studies: The Dialogue of Disciplines*, ed. Michael Harvey and Ronald E. Riggio (Cheltenham, United Kingdom: Edward Elgar, 2011), p. 20.
3. Howard Gardner, *Five Minds of the Future* (Boston, MA: Harvard Business Press, 2008), p. xiii.
4. See Steve Forbes and John Prevas, *Power, Ambition, Glory: The Stunning Parallels between Great Leaders of the Ancient World and Today . . . and The Lessons We Can Learn* (New York, NY: Three Rivers Press, 2009).

Conclusion

Leadership, for What?

"If the blind lead the blind, both shall fall in the ditch."
—Jesus Christ

Genovese Leadership Theorem: In any organization, unless stopped early, toxic people will multiply like rabbits—but aren't nearly as cute.

Leaders. There's been FDR and Hitler; Mandela and Mao; Lincoln and Pol Pot; Gandhi and Stalin; King Jr. and Indi Amir. Some have helped us reach out to the better angels within ourselves; others debased us and got us to debase ourselves. Leadership is essential, yet it can also be dangerous.

Throughout our lives, deliberately and accidentally, we will assume dozens and dozens of leadership roles. As parents and bosses, volunteers in a service organization, coach of a pee-wee soccer team, head of a food drive, organizer of a community watch program, we will be out there getting the job done.

Sometimes our acts of leadership will come at great pains and costs, as when we fail at a significant task, or stand up alone against injustice and face a hostile community. It takes a lot of courage to be a leader. And yet, is there a more noble act then to speak truth to power? Fight for justice? Give voice to the dispossessed? Bring hope to the hopeless?

Even more mundane (yet important) acts such as starting a small business, or organizing a charity bake sale, will test us in ways we could hardly imagine. If we thought hard and deep about the challenge ahead, we might not actually take the risk. But risk we do, every day in countless ways. We all show uncommon courage virtually every day of our lives. Leadership development can help us navigate the choppy waters of life's challenges. We will all be leaders in one way or another. Why not be better at it?

☐ Leadership: Necessary yet Potentially Dangerous

As discussed in Chapter 1 (The Dark Side), the lure of power or the need to "fix" yourself and your internal needs lead unhealthy people to seek out positions of leadership for all the wrong reasons. We should, thus, be wary and constantly on guard for would-be leaders too full of themselves or too hungry for power.

If leadership is necessary, it is also potentially dangerous. How do we keep leaders in check? One way is through humor.

One of the biggest fears for any leader—especially a politician—is that the public will laugh at them, and not with them. Just ask Sarah Palin. Is it even possible to think of Palin and not see Tina Fey's mocking—yet so very close to reality—parody of Palin? Today, Sarah Palin exists as little more than a caricature of herself. Humor hurts.

If imitation is the sincerest form of flattery, parody is the deepest slit of the throat. And in a television, YouTube, and cable era, political parody seems—to the politician at least—ubiquitous and can spread like a virus. Chevy Chase doing President Ford, Dan Akroyd doing Nixon, Dana Carvey as both George H. W. Bush and Ross Perot, John Hartman as Reagan, Darrell Hammond as Clinton, and of course, Will Ferrell as W, both on *Saturday Night Live* and in a one-man Broadway hit "You're Welcome America," all parodied and punctured their targets while imprinting on the minds of many, an image of bumbling buffoonery.

Although we have a long history of comically mocking our leaders—cartoons by Thomas Nast and Herblock, Mark Twain's classic short stories—today's media have been an especially effective means of dispensing the message to a national audience. And as hard news and soft entertainment seem increasingly to be merging (Saturday Night Live, The Daily Show, The Colbert Report), news has become entertainment, and entertainment, news.

We insist that our leaders pass the character test, and one measure of character is seen as having a good sense of humor as well as being able to take a joke and to laugh at yourself. Abraham Lincoln was widely known for his *stories*, humorous parables that also taught a lesson and helped humanize Lincoln. John Kennedy had a quick, ready wit that served him well in the early days of televised presidential news conferences. Ronald Reagan was a master of self-depreciating humor ("People say that hard work never killed anybody, but I say, why take the chance?") that offset criticism as well as endeared Reagan and the others to the public.

Indeed, we should be wary of people and presidents who do not exhibit a healthy sense of humor. Richard Nixon seemed absolutely humorless. One in-joke by Jimmy Carter's staff had it that "Carter's idea of self-deprecatory humor is to insult his staff."

In his collection of presidential humor, Gerald Gardner writes that:

> Bromidic as it may sound, humor is a most essential element in a democracy. Curiously, the one ingredient that totalitarian societies seem to have in common is a lack of humor. In a dictatorship the practice of satire is a jeopardous pastime indeed. This is doubtless because no public figure willingly subjects himself to the barbs of the satirist if there is some way to dispose of the troublesome fellow. In a democracy we cannot so readily eliminate our critics and iconoclasts.[1]

This is not altogether surprising. Humor can be a wounding weapon, and a persuasive one. The witty plays of George Bernard Shaw have proselytized more theatergoers than the grim narratives of Henrik Ibsen. So humor is considered subversive by the powers that be, who often pay it the compliment of suppression.

Humor is necessary in a democracy for reasons other than serving as a device for spreading truth and attacking fools and knaves. In a free society, every few years, the populace engages in a wrenching struggle for power. Humor lets us take the issues seriously without taking ourselves too seriously. If we are able to laugh at ourselves as we lunge for the jugular, the process loses some of its malice.

Laughing at politicians is as old as human memory. The Greek comic poets laughed and insulted Athenian politicians—to the delight of Athenian playgoers. Even the Bible says there's a time to laugh.

Freud, in his treatise on jokes and the unconscious, said jokes were a rebellion against authority, an often therapeutic venting toward, or mocking of, those in power. Humor, it is said, helps us cope with the painful and the forbidden and thus, at times, helps us cope in an unfair or mad world. Two British students of humor say we tell jokes because human existence can be so unforgiving. In their valuable *Only Joking*, Jimmy Carr and Lucy Greeves write: "Wherever human beings are oppressed—by corrupt government, poverty or merely the specter of disease and death—jokes thrive."[2]

We are ambivalent about leaders. We know someone has to solve public problems, forge policy compromises, and help govern our communities and nation-states. Yet most people rightly fear the abuse of power, think politics is often unsavory, and view most politicians as hopelessly unprincipled. In short, they are suspicious of power-wielding politicians. And writers from Machiavelli and Shakespeare to Mark Twain and George Orwell warn us about the guile, manipulation, and *double sidedness* inherent in the art of political leadership. Even at its best, politics is the skilled use of a blunt instrument. One way we deal with this is by laughing at politicians. We laugh at pretentiousness, hypocrisy, failures, and duplicity. Humor puts politicians on notice that we are watching and inherently distrustful, if not outright cynical. A good joke at the expense of a politician helps level the playing field. It helps prick pomposity and sappy sentimentality.[3]

Americans have a rich tradition of poking good, and sometimes piercing, fun at politicians. Every president has been skewered by comedians, caricaturists as well as by partisan activists. Mark Twain, Henry Adams, Will Rogers, H. L. Mencken, Bob Hope, Mort Sahl, and countless others including Art Buchwald and Molly Ivins all successfully made us laugh at politics and politicians. Further, the well-crafted cartoon by Thomas Nast or Herblock sometimes proves more of a rhetorical weapon than a rival's policy argument. Political humorists abound in today's 24/7 media culture. Thus Jay Leno, Jon Stewart, Garry Trudeau, Chris Rock, Dennis Miller, Stephen Colbert, and Bill Maher, among others, earn a splendid living making us laugh at Hillary and Bill, George W., Arnold, Barack Obama, and the rest.

Humor is a means of lighthearted (usually) fencing or even an unsubtle communication of disrespect toward politicians who seem to be always craving flattery. Who can help laugh (as well as cry) at Bill Clinton's squirming to explain his relationship with a White House intern, or at Republican leaders squirming about Congressman Mark Foley and his inappropriate advances toward congressional pages.

Another reason we laugh at politicians is because some of them actually are corrupt—corrupted by money it takes to win office, corrupted by bribes in office, and sometimes corrupted by power itself. Richard Nixon and his vice president, Spiro Agnew, are mainly remembered today for their various corruptions in office—and they are quite rightly satirized, ridiculed, and scorned. More recently, U.S. Representative Randy "Duke" Cunningham made millions for himself as he represented his San Diego area constituency by steering Defense Department and other federal agency contracts to grateful businesses who rewarded him in-kind. He now serves in jail and was one of the reasons Democrats retook the House of Representatives in the 2006 elections.

Thus laughing at wayward leaders is in some ways retribution, a punishment, scolding, and a way to get back at sleaze. By laughing at politicians, we are trying to warn them, letting them know what's acceptable and what's not. Clinton may not have been convicted when impeached over his lies about an external affair, but the countless jokes made at his expense reminded him that we are not entirely accepting of what he did. Irreverent humor can help demystify and check some of the unacceptable behaviors of corrupt politicians.

We laugh at politicians because politics can be extremely serious. Yet humor can relieve some of the tension that is all too present in public affairs. The effective politician had to be able to take a joke and to tell jokes about his or her own mistakes to let people know he or she is human. A politician who can poke fun at him- or herself earns our respect.

Few things are worse for a politician than to be called "humorless" or worse "absolutely humorless." Ralph Nader, Jimmy Carter, and Richard Nixon were so tagged. "He's just a total joke" might be even more damaging. Still, Will Rogers repeatedly warned, "the problem with jokes is they often get elected." Most people are bored and bewildered by politics and politicians. Lawmaking, policymaking, and diplomacy are slow moving, tedious, and hard to follow. Political humor typically focuses on the negative. Unattractive foibles, traits as well as lies and mistakes invite joking. We want to laugh at misery, at failure, at sleaze, so as to lessen its affect on us. Negativity is simply more interesting to us than positive news. This is why negative ads and campaigns, sadly, work so well. Thus the sinister refrain in recent elections, "If you can't say anything nice about a candidate, by god, let's hear it!"

Rarely a day goes by that rival politicians aren't accusing one another of being "political." You don't hear doctors accusing one another of being "medical," or a good writer accusing a fellow colleague of "being a writer."

☐ Leadership, for What?

Much has been written about the "crisis of leadership" in the United States. Former Chrysler CEO Lee Iacocca's 2008 book entitled *Where Have All the Leaders Gone?*[4] taps into a recurring theme in modern America.

Although it often seems as if we live in a world where no one is in charge, in truth, we have many outstanding men and women willing to serve society. Our goal is to identify the best among them, find ways to lend them our support, and give them the tools (skills) necessary for effective leadership.

And we can never lose sight of the fact that leadership is about ends: achieving group goals. Robert Frost once said, "Poetry is about the grief. Politics is about the grievance." We must keep in mind what Mohandas K. Gandhi called the seven social sins: "politics without principle, wealth without work, commerce without morality, pleasure without conscience, education without character, science without humanity, and worship without sacrifice."[5]

☐ Things We Tell Our Students

Several years ago, my mentor, friend, and frequent coauthor, Thomas E. Cronin, and I were driving from Albuquerque to Santa Fe, New Mexico when he said, "Take out a piece of paper"—which I did—"and let's write down the things we tell our students about leadership." "So you mean," I asked, "the 'leadership lessons' we tell them?" "Yes," he said, and herewith, the list:

Leadership Lessons:

- Be a generalist.
- Leadership *can* be learned.
- Know thyself.
- The unexamined life is not worth living.
- Learn from your weaknesses and learn to compensate for them.
- Embrace failure, learn from your failures.
- Good judgment is the key.
- Curiosity didn't kill the cat, stupidity did.
- Take responsibility, don't blame someone else.
- You need to *like* people and like yourself.
- Committees may be frustrating, but they are important.
- Diversity is not a burden, it is an opportunity.
- Set and reach goals.
- Don't procrastinate.
- Make a list of things to do each day—and do them!
- Be organized.
- Rely on evidence not wishful thinking.
- Control your anger.
- Learn finance, budgeting, and accounting.

- Read the classics (Homer, Plutarch, Plato, Aristotle, Machiavelli, the great thinkers, and of course . . . Shakespeare and the Bible).
- Leaders are people who see something that needs to be done and get it done.
- Context matters.
- Be proactive even when reacting.
- Learn to delegate wisely.
- Develop emotional intelligence.
- Travel, travel, travel.
- Have a sense of humor (especially about yourself . . . or, take what you do seriously, but not yourself).
- Be optimistic.
- Work to cultivate luck.
- Phronesis!!!
- Give/serve others.
- Empathy is (almost) everything.
- Get a puppy.
- Self-confidence.
- Be cautiously bold.
- Self-control/self-discipline.
- Creativity counts.
- You elevate yourself by serving others.
- Always rise above it.
- Be quick to praise, slow to criticize.
- Always seek what your "better angels" would have you do.
- Lift as you climb.
- Call your mom.
- Lennon and McCartney were right, "The love you take is equal to the love you make."

☐ The Way Forward

As Eric Hoffer noted, "Precisely a society that can get along without leaders is the one that's producing leaders."[6] Effective leaders empower others, create a cadre of leaders. In the end, the less the leader *needs* to do, the better off everyone is. But the need for leadership declines only as *we* take greater responsibility and leadership in our communities. We cannot live without leaders, but we must create conditions in which our leaders *need* to do less. When we rely on leaders, we cede power and responsibility to others. Some granting of authority and power is necessary. Yet do we give away too much?

In his play, *Life of Galileo,* one of Bertolt Brecht's characters says, "Unhappy is the land that has no heroes," to which Galileo replies, "No. Unhappy is the land that needs heroes." Who is correct? What role do heroes, role models, celebrities, and those above us play in the development of our identities and in the practice of democracy?

Clearly if we worship heroes we see ourselves as beneath them. This can't be good for us, and it is disastrous for democracy. Worship, no. But what of those who serve as positive role models or who possess honorable traits that we might model? We can admire Gandhi for his nonviolence yet not worship him as a god. So yes, we need role models, but heroes pose particular problems. It is difficult to be critical of our heroes; we may excuse a great deal when our hero does something unsavory. And hero-worship is especially dangerous in a democracy when the people are to be the ultimate bosses.

During his campaign for president in 1968, Robert F. Kennedy challenged the status quo definition of what was good (merely a high gross national product, GNP) by asking us to reconceptualize our values. He said:

> Too much and too long, we seem to have surrendered community excellence and community values in the mere accumulation of material things. Our gross national product . . . if we should judge America by that—counts air pollution and cigarette advertising, and ambulances to clear our highways of carnage. It counts special locks for our doors and the jails for those who break them. It counts the destruction of our redwoods and the loss of our natural wonder in chaotic sprawl. It counts napalm and the cost of a nuclear warhead, and armored cars for police who fight riots in our streets. It counts Whitman's rifle and Speck's knife, and the television programs which glorify violence in order to sell toys to our children.
>
> Yet the gross national product does not allow for the health of our children, the quality of their education, or the joy of their play. It does not include the beauty of our poetry or the strength of our marriages; the intelligence of our public debate or the integrity of our public officials. It measures neither our wit nor our courage; neither our wisdom nor our learning; neither our compassion nor our devotion to our country; it measures everything, in short, except that which makes life worthwhile. And it tells us everything about America except why we are proud that we are Americans.[7]

And finally, listen to your mother! There is great wisdom there, and if you fail to absorb that wisdom, you may end up like Arthur in *The Hitchhiker's Guide to the Galaxy*:

Arthur: It's times like this I wish I'd listen to my mother.
Ford: Why, what did she say?
Arthur: I don't know, I never listened.[8]

☐ NOTES

1. Gerald Gardner, *The Mocking of the President* (New York, NY: Harper & Row, 1989), pp. xi–xx.
2. Carr and Greeves, *Only Joking* (New York, NY: Gotham, 2006).
3. This section draws on the pioneering work on political humor by Thomas E. Cronin, who has generously allowed me to borrow from his work.
4. Lee Iacocca, *Where Have All the Leaders Gone?* (New York, NY: Scribner's, 2008).
5. Jim Wallis, *The Soul of Politics: Beyond "Religious Right" and "Secular Left"* (New York, NY: Mariner Books, 1995), p. xiii.
6. Eric Hoffer, "Interview with Eric Sevareid," *CBS Television*, September 19, 1967.
7. Robert F. Kennedy, "Public Address," University of Kansas, Kansas, March 18, 1968.
8. Douglas Adams, *The Hitchhiker's Guide to the Galaxy*, 25th ed. (New York, NY: Crown, 2004).

AUTHOR INDEX

Note: Page numbers in *italics* indicate tables or figures.

A

Acton, Lord 18
Adams, Henry 18, 104
Adams, William C. *54*
Agnew, Spiro 104
Akroyd, Dan 102
Albrion, Mitch 100
Alinsky, Saul 90–1
Al-Jazari 5
Al-Sadig, Jafar 5
Aristotle xiii, 4, 6–7, 15, 37, 40–1, 47,
    50, 63, 78
Asimov, Isaac 1
Auden, W. H. 81
Augustus 87
Aurelius, Marcus 82

B

Beckett, Samuel 75
Bennis, Warren xii–xiii, 70, 99
Berra, Yogi 72
Bird, Larry 28
Bonaparte, Napoleon 60, 93
Brecht, Bertolt 108
Bruns, Brianna xiii
Buchanan, James 8
Buchwald, Art 104
Buffett, Warren 22
Burns, James M. xii, 8, 99
Burr, Mackenzie xiii
Bush, George H. W. 102
Bush, George W. 23, 25, 59, 67,
    76, 77

C

Caesar, Julius 5
Camus, Albert 23
Candau, Matt xiii
Carlson, Richard 68–9
Carlyle, Thomas 7–8
Caro, Robert 100
Carr, Jimmy 103
Carter, Jimmy 24, 74, 103, 105

Carvey, Dana 102
Castracani, Castruccio 96
Chase, Chevy 102
Churchill, Winston 25
Cicero 67–8, 94
Ciulla, Joanne B. 94
Clinton, Bill 23, 25, 75, 104
Colbert, Stephen 104
Conners, Jimmy 28
Cronin, Thomas E. xiii, 3, *18*, 20, 83,
    100, 106
Cunningham, Randy "Duke" 104–5

D

Darwin, Charles 67
da Vinci, Leonardo 5
Disraeli, Benjamin 31
Drucker, Peter xiii, 100

E

Eastwood, Clint 22
Edison, Thomas 22, 75
Einstein, Albert 81
Eliot, T. S. 29
Emerson, Ralph Waldo 7, 60, 82
Erasmus 43, 46

F

Federer, Roger 28
Ferrell, Will 102
Finzel, Hans 100
Fisher, Roger 100
Flavell, J. H. 88
Foley, Mark 104
Ford, Gerald 76
Ford, Harrison 22
Frost, Robert 106

G

Gandhi, Mohandas K. 23, 101, 106, 108
Gardner, Gerald 103
Gardner, Howard 30, 95

Gardner, John W. xiii, 99
Gates, Bill 22, 73
Genovese, Michael *18*, 100
Goleman, Daniel 63, 100
Gracian, Balthezar 60, 61
Greeves, Lucy 103

H

Hamilton, Alexander 57, 99
Hammond, Darrell 102
Hartley, Rebecca xiii
Hartman, John 102
Harvey, Michael 3–4
Havel, Vaclev 73
Heifetz, Ron 73
Herblock (Herbert Lawrence Block)
    102, 104
Hesburgh, Theodore 73
Hesse, Herman 100
Hitchcock, Alfred 22
Hodges, Albert G. 8
Hoffer, Eric 107
Hogan, Kevin 85
Holt, John 89
Hope, Bob 104
Hugo, Victor 72–3

I

Iacocca, Lee 105
Ibsen, Henrik 100, 103
Ivins, Molly 104

J

Jay, John 99
Jefferson, Thomas 5, 31–2
Jesus Christ of Nazareth 73, 101
Jeter, Derek 28, 63–4, 65, 98
Jobs, Steve 23
Johnson, Lyndon B. 91
Jordan, Michael 22, 28, 65
Joyce, Mary Ellen *54*
Juvenal 39

K

Kahnweiler, Jennifer B. 22
Kellerman, Barbara xii
Kennedy, John F. 5, 25, 31, 72, 76, 91,
    102–3
Kennedy, Robert F. 108
Keohane, Nan 58

King, Martin Luther, Jr. 6, 18, 19, 22, 23,
    72, 91, 96, 101
Kingdom, John 83
Kotter, John 90

L

Lawrence, T. E. 73
Lee, Harper 100
Lehrer, Jonah 58, 87, 100
Leno, Jay 104
Lewinsky, Monica 76
Lincoln, Abraham 8, 22, 25, 73, 96,
    102
Lombardi, Vince 27–8

M

Machiavelli, Niccolo xiii, 2, 17, 37,
    42–5, 47, 61, 67, 96, 99, 104
Madison, James 99
Maher, Bill 104
Mandela, Nelson 73, 96, 100
Martin, Steve 22
Marx, Karl 8
Mayer, John D. 62
McGrath, Katherine xiii
McLelland, David 15
Mencken, H. L. 104
Merkel, Angela 13
Michels, Robert 3
Miller, Dennis 104
Miroff, Bruce 100
Mother Teresa 22

N

Nader, Ralph 105
Nast, Thomas 102, 104
Newton, Isaac 5
Nixon, Richard 25, 70, 75, 102, 103,
    104, 105
Nye, Joseph S., Jr. 77–8

O

Obama, Barack 22, 24
O'Neill, Eugene 29
Orwell, George 104

P

Paine, Thomas 23, 81
Palin, Sarah 102

Pele 28
Perot, Ross 102
Plato xiii, 2, 37–40, 44, 47
Player, Gary 60
Plimpton, George 28
Plutarch 2, 61, 95–6
Provizer, Norman 8, 9

R

Reagan, Ronald 24, 71, 75, 103
Richelieu, Cardinal 42, 72
Rock, Chris 104
Rogers, Will 104, 105
Romney, Mitt 22
Roosevelt, Franklin D. 68, 96
Roosevelt, Theodore 5, 96
Rossiter, Clinton 84
Russell, Bertrand 42

S

Sahl, Mort 104
St. Francis of Assisi 37
Sakharov, Andrai 96
Salovey, Peter 62
Sample, Steven 7–8
Schwarzkopf, Norman 17
Shakespeare, William xiii, 37, 45–7, 104
Shaw, George Bernard 29–30, 103
Simonton, Dean Keith 8

Socrates 37, 40
Starr, Bart 27–8
Stewart, Jon 104
Sun Tzu 68
Syrus, Publilius 49

T

Thorndike, E. L. 62
Tillius, Marcus 94
Tolstoy, Leo 7
Toqueville, Alexis de 8
Trudeau, Garry 104
Tuchman, Barbara 100
Twain, Mark 102, 104

U

Ury, William L. 100
U.S. Office of Personnel Management 55

W

Weber, Max 1
Wechsler, D. 62
Welch, Jack 86
Westin, Drew 100
Whitman, Walt 87–8
Wooden, John 64, 100
Woodruff, Paul 100
Wren, J. Thomas 100

SUBJECT INDEX

Note: Page numbers in *italics* indicate tables or figures.

A

accident of birth stage 49–50
achievement 15, 23
adaptation 73–5
affiliate 15
agency in leadership studies 7–9
anarchy 37, 40, 45
aristocracy 40
Aristotle 40–2
"Aristotle's Metaphysics" 6
art of being lucky 60
Art of War, The (Sun Tzu) 68

B

balance 57, 67–9
blind optimism 75
bounded rationality 59, 87, 88
brain science 58
breathing exercises, yoga and 69

C

Candidate, The (movie) 16
causation in leadership studies 7–9
change 8; *see also* leadership change; organizational change
character quotient *65*, 66
Civil Service Commission 51; General Checklist of Executive Qualifications 52–6
cognitive skills 63
committees, leadership in/of 98–9
communication skills 57
community organizing 97
compass, moral courage and 69–70
concentration, yoga and 69
constitutional dictator 84
contextual intelligence 77–8
Coriolanus (Shakespeare) 46
courage: as leadership competency 51; leadership training and 39; moral 69–70; polymath leader and 3

D

decision-making: bounded rationality and 59, 87–8; challenges 59–60; factors used to make *58*; framing and 59; group think and 59; hubris and 59; individual 59; inputs *58*; judgment and 58–9; organizational 60; rational brain *vs.* emotional brain and 58; traps 59
demands of leaders 20–1
Democracy in America (Toqueville) 8
democratic distemper, globalism and 13–15
Discourses, The (Machiavelli) 42, 45
double sidedness 104

E

early childhood development stage 50
emotional intelligence 62–6
empathy 66–7
environmental crisis 74
ethical guidelines, yoga and 69
Eudiamonia 41
Executive Core Qualifications (OPM) 55–6
executive function 65–6
experience quotient *65*, 66
experience stage 50–1
extroverts *see* introverts and extroverts as leaders

F

failure, success of 90
flexibility 57, 67–9
focus, yoga and 68–9
forces of history, Great Man Theory *vs.* 7–9
framing 59

G

gender, leadership and 26–7, *26*
General Checklist of Executive Qualifications (Civil Service Commission) 51

Genovese Leadership Academy
93–100; leadership composites and
95–6; leadership essentials and
96–7; leadership in/of committees
and 98–9; liberal arts education
training 93–5; life as a teacher and
97–8; mentors and role models
and 99
Genovese Leadership Theorems 1, 37,
49, 81, 93, 101
globalization: democratic distemper
and 13–15; described 10–12;
leadership and 9–13; technological
innovations and 10, 11
golden mean 40, 41, 50
government: crisis 84; globalism and
12, 15; judgment and
57; necessity of 4; in Plato's
Politics 40; technological
innovations and 11
Great Man Theory *vs.* forces of history
7–9
group think 59
guile 61, 104

H

Hamlet (Shakespeare) 47
happiness, yoga and 69
happiness of leader 19–20
high-flex 12, 67
high-flux 12, 67
hubris 59
humor 102–5

I

Index Librorum Prohitorum
(Machiavelli) 42
informed optimism 75
insanity 81
insiders 23
intelligence quotient (IQ) 65, 66
inter-/intrapersonal skills 71
internships 97
introverts and extroverts as leaders
21–6; characteristics of 22; examples
of famous 22–3; as insiders or
outsiders 23; introvert/extrovert
continuum, dimensions of 25;
in populations and leadership
positions 22
iron law of oligarchy 3

J

journey to maturity stage 50
judgment 57–61
Julius Caesar (Shakespeare) 46

K

kingship 40

L

leaderless movements 14
leaders: building (*see* Genovese
Leadership Academy);
characteristics of 18; demands of
20–1; dysfunctional 30–1; happiness
of 19–20; introverts and extroverts
as 21–6; misdiagnosing the problem
74; motivations for being 15–17, 16;
polymath 4–5; power's effect on
29–30; of tomorrow, building 9
leadership: adaptive function of,
change and 86–7; changing nature
of 13, 15; components of 6; defining
5–6; essentials of 96–7; gender
and 26–7, 26; globalization and
9–13; happiness of leader and
19–20; importance of 1–4; in/of
committees 98–9; lessons 106–7;
metaphysics of 6–7; myths about 3;
vs. power 17–18; principles of 7; six
Qs of 65, 65; skills 63; sports and
27–8; studies, agency and causation
in 7–9; training 2, 4, 51, 71–2, 93, 94
leadership change 81–91; adaptive
function of leadership and 86–7;
attraction of 85–6; bounded
rationality and 87–9; Machiavelli
and 82–5; organizational 89–90;
success of failure in 90
leadership competencies 45–53
leadership composites 37–47; Aristotle
40–2; Genovese Leadership
Academy and 93; Machiavelli 42–5,
96; Plato 37–40; Plutarch 61, 95–6;
Shakespeare 45–7
Leadership Effectiveness Framework
(OPM) 55
leadership learning, stages of
49–51; accident of birth 49–50;
early childhood development
50; experience 50–1; journey to
maturity 50

leadership toolkit: adaptation 73–5; communication skills 71; contextual intelligence 77–8; emotional intelligence 62–6; empathy 66–7; flexibility and balance 67–9; judgment 57–61; leadership competencies 49–57; moral courage and compass 69–70; self-knowledge/world knowledge 70–1; setbacks and mistakes 75–7; talent 71–2; vision, articulating 72–3
learned optimism 75
liberal arts education quotient 65, 66
liberal arts education training 93–5
life as a teacher 97–8
Life of Alexander (Plutarch) 96
Life of Caesar (Plutarch) 96
Life of Galileo (Brecht) 108
Life of Romulus (Plutarch) 96
Life of Theseus (Plutarch) 96
luck 43–4, 60–1, 73, 77, 97

M

Machiavelli, Niccolo 42–5, 82–5, 96
Machiavellianism 42, 44
Management Excellence Framework (OPM) 53–4
manipulation 45, 46, 104
meditation, yoga and 69
Meditations (Aurelius) 82
mentors 97
metacognition 59, 88
metaphysics of leadership 6–7
mistakes 75–7
monarchy 40, 46
motivation 15

N

nature and nurture 49, 71
Nicomachean Ethics (Aristotle) 41
Notes on the State of Virginia (Jefferson) 31

O

Office of Personnel Management (OPM) 51; Executive Core Qualifications 55–6; Leadership Effectiveness Framework 55; Management Excellence Framework 53–4
oligarchy 3, 40

On Becoming a Leader (Bennis) 70
Only Joking (Carr and Greeves) 103
openness 54, 59
opportunities, success and 60
optimism 24, 25, 60; blind 75; informed 75; learned 75
organizational change 90–1; confronting 89–90; principles of 90–1; success of failure in 90
organizational decision-making 59
outsiders 23

P

philosopher-king 2, 37–9, 40
phronesis 41–2, 47
Plato 37–40
Plutarch 2, 61, 95–6
politicians: *The Art of War* and 68; laughing at 103–4; qualities of 1–2
politics: defining 5; devotion to 2; scientific basis of 57–8; Shakespeare's 45, 46; style-flex and 67–8
Politics (Aristotle) 40, 41
polymath, defined 4
polymath leader: committee assignment and 98–9; described 4–5; examples of famous 4–5; portrait of 31–2
power: effect of, on leaders 29–30; leadership *vs.* 17–18
Prince, The (Machiavelli) 2, 42–5, 61, 82, 96
prudence 39, 42, 43

R

recognizing talent 71–2
Republic, The (Plato) 37–9
rewarding talent 71–2
rigidity 67
Rise and Fall of Athens, The (Plutarch) 61
role models 99

S

self-awareness 47, 58, 59, 62–3, 65, 77, 78
self-knowledge 70–1
setbacks 75–7
seven social sins 106
Shakespeare, William 45–7

social intelligence 62
"Song of Myself" (Whitman) 87–8
style-flex 26, 67
success: of failure 90; opportunities
 and 60–1

T

talent 71–2
technical skills 63
technological innovations
 10, 11
thinking, keys to 59
trait theory 66
tyranny 37, 40, 46

U

United States as superpower 11

V

vision, articulating 72–3

W

window of opportunity 61
world knowledge 70–1

Y

yoga 68–9; limbs of 69